SELECT DEMONSTRATIONS

APHRAHAT

A E T E R N A   P R E S S

PUBLISHED BY AETERNA PRESS.
COVER DESIGN BY AETERNA PRESS.

GREGORY THE GREAT (II), EPHRAIM SYRUS, APHRAHAT CREATOR(S): SCHAFF, PHILIP (1819–1893) (EDITOR).

ISBN-13: 978-1-78516-907-6

AVAILABLE AS AN E-BOOK:
WWW.AETERNAPRESS.COM

CONTENTS

Aphrahat

Letter of an Inquirer

1. Beloved, I send thee inquiries and questions, for I am compelled to seek further instruction of thee on many points. Do not thou refuse to hear me. My spirit urges me to warn thee about many topics that thou mayest unfold for me the spiritual perceptions of thy mind, and mayest show me of all that thou hast apprehended from the holy books, that so my deficiency may be supplied by thee and my hunger satisfied by thy doctrine, and that thou mayest assuage my thirst from the fountain of thine instruction. Yet though many things are set in my thought to ask thee, they all are notwithstanding reserved with me, that when I come to thee, thou mayest instruct me on all subjects.

2. But before all things I desire that thou wouldst write and instruct me concerning this that straitens me, namely, concerning our faith; how it is, and what its foundation is, and on what structure it rises, on what it rests, and in what way is its fulfilment and consummation, and what are the works required for it. For I of myself firmly believe that God is one, Who made the heavens and the earth from the beginning; that He adorned the world by His handiwork; that He made man in His image; He it is that accepted the offering of Abel. He translated Enoch because of his excellence. He preserved Noah because of his righteousness. He chose Abraham because of his faith. He spake with Moses on account of his meekness. He it is that spake in all the prophets, and furthermore He sent His Christ into the world. Since then, my brother, I thus believe in these things that so they are, I therefore, brother, request of thee that thou wouldest write and show me what are the works required for this our faith, that so thou mayest set me at rest.

Demonstration I

Of Faith

1. I have received thy letter, my beloved, and when I read it, it greatly gladdened me that thou hast turned thy thoughts to these investigations. For this thing that thou hast asked of me shall be freely granted, for freely it was received. And whosoever has, and desires to withhold from him that seeks, whatsoever he withholds shall be taken away from him. Whoever of free grace receives, of free grace also does it behove him to give. And so, my beloved, as to that which thou hast asked of me, so far as my insignificance has apprehended, I will write to thee. And also whatsoever thou hast not sought of me, invoking God, I will explain to thee. Hear then, my beloved, and open the inward ears of thy heart unto me, and the spiritual perceptions of thy mind to that which I say unto thee.

2. Faith is compounded of many things, and by many kinds is it brought to perfection. For it is like a building that is built up of many pieces of workmanship and so its edifice rises to the top. And know, my beloved, that in the foundations of the building stones are laid, and so resting upon stones the whole edifice rises until it is perfected. Thus also the true Stone, our Lord Jesus Christ, is the foundation of all our faith. And on Him, on [this] Stone faith is based. And resting on faith all the structure rises until it is completed. For it is the foundation that is the beginning of all the building. For when any one is brought nigh unto faith, it is laid for him upon the Stone, that is our Lord Jesus Christ. And his building cannot be shaken by the waves, nor can it be injured by the winds. By the stormy blasts it does not fall, because its structure is reared upon the rock of the true Stone. And in this that I have called Christ the Stone, I have not spoken of my own thought, but the Prophets beforehand called Him the Stone. And this I shall make clear to thee.

3. And now hear concerning faith that is based upon the Stone, and concerning the structure that is reared up upon the Stone. For first a man believes,

and when he believes, he loves. When he loves, he hopes. When he hopes, he is justified. When he is justified, he is perfected. When he is perfected, he is consummated. And when his whole structure is raised up, consummated, and perfected, then he becomes a house and a temple for a dwelling-place of Christ, as Jeremiah the Prophet said:—The temple of the Lord, the temple of the Lord, the temple of the Lord are ye, if ye amend your ways and your works. And again He said through the Prophet:—I will dwell in them and walk in them. And also the Blessed Apostle thus said:—Ye are the temple of God and the spirit of Christ dwelleth in you. And also our Lord again thus said to His disciples:—Ye are in Me and I am in you.

4. And when the house has become a dwelling-place, then the man begins to be anxious as to that which is required for Him Who dwells in the building. Just as if a king or an honourable man, to whom a royal name is given, should lodge in the house, there would be required for the King all the appurtenances of royalty and all the service that is needed for the King's honour. For in a house that is void of all good things, the King will not lodge, nor will he dwell in the midst of it; but all that is choicest in the house is required for the King and that nothing in it be deficient. And if anything be deficient there in the house in which the King lodges, the keeper of the house is delivered over to death, because he did not make ready the service for the King. So also let the man, who becomes a house, yea a dwelling-place, for Christ, take heed to what is needed for the service of Christ, Who lodges in him, and with what things he may please Him. For first he builds his building on the Stone, which is Christ. On Him, on the Stone, is faith based, and on faith is reared up all the structure. For the habitation of the house is required pure fasting, and it is made firm by faith. There is also needed for it pure prayer, and through faith is it accepted. Necessary for it too is love, and with faith is it compounded. Furthermore alms are needed, and through faith are they given. He demands also meekness, and by faith is it adorned. He chooses too virginity, and by faith is it loved. He joins with himself holiness, and in faith is it planted. He cares also for wisdom, and through faith is it acquired. He desires also hospitality, and by faith does it abound. Requisite for Him also is simplicity, and with faith is it commingled. He demands patience also, and by faith is it perfected. He has respect also to long-suffering, and through faith is it acquired. He loves mourning also, and through faith is it manifested. He seeks also for purity, and by faith is it preserved. All these things does the faith demand that is based on the rock of the true Stone, that is Christ. These works are required for Christ the King, Who dwells in men that are built up in these works.

5. And if perchance thou shouldest say:—If Christ is set for the foundation, how does Christ also dwell in the building when it is completed? For both these things did the blessed Apostle say. For he said:—I as a wise architect have laid the foundation. And there he defined the foundation and made it clear, for he said as follows:—No man can lay other foundation than that which is laid, which is Jesus Christ. And that Christ furthermore dwells in that building is the word that was written above—that of Jeremiah who called men temples and said of God that He dwelt in them. And the Apostle said:—The Spirit of Christ dwelleth in you. And our Lord said:—I and My Father are one. And therefore that word is accomplished, that Christ dwells in men, namely, in those who believe on Him, and He is the foundation on which is reared up the whole building.

6. But I must proceed to my former statement that Christ is called the Stone in the Prophets. For in ancient times David said concerning Him:—The stone which the builders rejected has become the head of the building. And how did the builders reject this Stone which is Christ? How else than that they so rejected Him before Pilate and said—This man shall not be King over us. And again in that parable that our Lord spake that a certain nobleman went to receive kingly power and to return and rule over them; and they sent after Him envoys saying:—This man shall not be King over us. By these things they rejected the Stone which is Christ. And how did it become the head of the building? How else than that it was set up over the building of the Gentiles and upon it is reared up all their building. And who are the builders? Who but the priests and Pharisees who did not build a sure building, but were overthrowing everything that he was building, as is written in Ezekiel the Prophet:—He was building a wall of partition, but they were shaking it, that it might fall. And again it is written:—I sought amongst them a man who was closing the fence and standing in the breach over the face of the land, that I might not destroy it and I did not find. And furthermore Isaiah also prophesied beforehand with regard to this stone. For he said:—Thus saith the Lord, Behold I lay in Zion a chosen stone in the precious corner, the heart of the wall of the foundation. And he said again there:—Every one that believeth on it shall not fear. And whosoever falleth on that stone shall be broken, and every one on whom it shall fall, it will crush. For the people of the house of Israel fell upon Him, and He became their destruction for ever. And again it shall fall on the image and crush it. And the Gentiles believed on it and do not fear.

7. And He shows thus with regard to that stone that it was laid as head of the wall and as foundation. But if that stone was laid as the foundation, how did it also become the head of the wall? How but that when our Lord came,

He laid His faith in the earth like a foundation, and it rose above all the heavens like the head of the wall and all the building was finished with the stones, from the bottom to the top. And with regard to the faith about which I said that He laid His faith in the earth, this David proclaimed beforehand about Christ. For He said:—Faith shall spring up from the earth. And that again, it is above, he said:—Righteousness looked down from the heavens.

8. And again Daniel also spoke concerning this stone which is Christ. For he said:—The stone was cut out from the mountain, not by hands, and it smote the image, and the whole earth was filled with it. This he showed beforehand with regard to Christ that the whole earth shall be filled with Him. For lo! by the faith of Christ are all the ends of the earth filled, as David said:—The sound of the Gospel of Christ has gone forth into all the earth. And again when He sent forth His apostles He spake thus to them:—Go forth, make disciples of all nations and they will believe on Me. And again the Prophet Zechariah also prophesied about that stone which is Christ. For he said:—I saw a chief stone of equality and of love. And why did he say "chief"? Surely because from the beginning He was with His Father. And again that he spoke of love, it was because when He came into the world, He said thus to His disciples:—This is My commandment, that ye love one another. And again He said:—I have called you My friends (lovers). And the blessed Apostle said thus:—God loved as in the love of His Son. Of a truth Christ loved us and gave Himself for us.

9. And definitely did He show concerning this stone:—Lo! on this stone will I open seven eyes. And what then are the seven eyes that were opened on the stone? Clearly the Spirit of God that abode on Christ with seven operations, as Isaiah the Prophet said:—The Spirit of God shall rest and dwell upon Him, (a spirit) of wisdom and understanding, of counsel and of courage, of knowledge and of the fear of the Lord. These were the seven eyes that were opened upon the Stone, and these are the seven eyes of the Lord which look upon all the earth.

10. And also with reference to Christ was this (which follows) said. For he said that He was given as a light to all the Gentiles as the Prophet Isaiah said:—I have given Thee as a light to all the Gentiles, that Thou shouldest be My redemption to the ends of the earth. And furthermore David also said;—Thy word is a lamp unto my feet and a light unto my paths. And also the word and discourse of the Lord is Christ, as is written in the beginning of the Gospel of our Saviour:—In the beginning was the Word. And with regard to the light there again he bore witness:—The light was shining in the darkness and the darkness comprehended it not. What then is this:—The light was shining in

the darkness and the darkness comprehended it not? Clearly Christ, Whose light shone in the midst of the people of the house of Israel, and the people of the house of Israel did not comprehend the light of Christ, in that they did not believe on Him, as it is written:—He came unto His own, and His own received Him not. And also our Lord Jesus called them darkness, for He said to His disciples;—Whatsoever I say unto you in the darkness, that speak ye in the light, namely, let your light shine among the Gentiles; because they received the light of Christ, Who is the Light of the Gentiles. And He said again to His Apostles:—Ye are the light of the world. And again He said unto them;—Let your light shine before men, that they may see your good works and glorify your Father which is in heaven. And again He showed with regard to Himself that He is the light, for He said to His disciples:—Walk while the light is with you, ere the darkness overtake you. And again He said to them:—Believe on the light that ye may be children of light. And again He said:—I am the light of the world. And again He said:—No man lighteth a lamp and putteth it under a bushel or under a bed, or putteth it in a hidden place, but putteth it upon the lamp-stand that every one may see the light of the lamp. And the shining lamp is Christ, as David said;—Thy word is a lamp unto my feet and a light to my paths.

11. And furthermore the Prophet Hosea also said:—Light you a lamp and seek ye the Lord. And our Lord Jesus Christ said:—What woman is there who has ten drachmos and shall lose one of them, and will not light a lamp and sweep the house and seek her drachma that she lost? What then does this woman signify? Clearly the congregation of the house of Israel, to which the ten commandments were given. They lost the first commandment—that in which He warned them saying:—I am the Lord your God, Who brought you up from the land of Egypt. And when they had lost this first commandment, also the nine which are after it they could not keep, because on the first depend the nine. For it was an impossibility that while worshipping Baal, they should keep the nine commandments. For they lost the first commandment, like that woman who lost one drachma from the ten. So the Prophet cried unto them:—Light you a lamp and seek ye the Lord. And furthermore the Prophet Isaiah also said:—Seek ye the Lord and when ye shall have found Him, call upon Him; and when He is near let the sinner abandon his way and the wicked man his thought. For that lamp shone and they did not by it seek the Lord their God. And its light shone in the darkness and the darkness did not comprehend it. And the lamp was set up on the lamp-stand and those who were in the house did not see its light. And what then means this, that the lamp was set up on the lamp-stand? Clearly His being raised up upon the cross. And by this

all the house was made dark over them. For when they crucified Him, the light was darkened from them, and shone amongst the Gentiles, because that from the time of the sixth hour (of the day) on which they crucified Him even unto the ninth hour there was darkness in all the land of Israel. And the sun set in midday and the land was darkened in the shining daytime, as is written in Zechariah the Prophet:—It shall come to pass in that day, saith the Lord, I will cause the sun to set in midday, and will make dark the land in the shining daytime.

12. Now I must proceed to my former subject of faith, that on it are reared up all the good works of the building. And again, in what I said with regard to the building, it was in no strange fashion that I spoke, but the blessed Apostle wrote in the first Epistle to the Corinthians, saying;—I as a wise master-builder have laid the foundation, but every one buildeth on it. One builds silver and gold and goodly stones; another builds reed and straw and stubble. In the last day that building shall be tried by fire; for the gold and silver and goodly stones shall be preserved in the midst of the fire, because they are a firm building. But as for the straw and reed and stubble, the fire shall have power upon them and they shall be burned. And what is the gold and silver and goodly stones by which the building is raised up? Clearly the good deeds of faith, which shall be preserved in the midst of the fire; because Christ dwells in that secure building, and He is its preserver from the fire. And let us consider and understand (this) from the example that God has given us also in the former dispensation, because the promises of that dispensation will abide sure for us. Let us then understand from (the case of) those three righteous men who were cast into the midst of the fire and were not burned, namely, Hananiah, Azariah and Misael, over whom the fire had no power, because they built a secure building and rejected the commandment of Nebuchadnezzar the king and did not worship the image that he made. And as for those who transgressed the commandment of God, the fire at once prevailed over them and burned them, and they were burned without mercy. For the Sodomites were burned like straw and reed and stubble. Furthermore, Nadab and Abihu were burned, who transgressed the commandment of God. Again, two hundred and fifty men were burned, who were offering incense. Again, two princes and a hundred who were with them were burned, because they approached the mountain on which Elijah was sitting, who ascended in a chariot of fire to heaven. The calumniators also were burned because they dug a pit for righteous men. Accordingly, beloved, the righteous shall be tried by the fire, like gold and silver and goodly stones, and the wicked shall be burned in the fire like straw and reed and stubble, and the fire shall have power upon them and they shall

be burned; even as the Prophet Isaiah said:—By fire shall the Lord judge and by it shall He try all flesh. And again he said:—Ye shall go out and see the carcases of the men who offended against Me, whose worm shall not die, nor shall their fire be quenched, and they shall be an astonishment to all flesh.

13. And again the Apostle has commented for us upon this building and upon this foundation; for he said thus;—No man can lay another foundation than that which is laid, which is Jesus Christ. Again the Apostle said about faith that it is conjoined with hope and love, for he said thus:—These are three which shall abide, faith and hope and love. And he showed with regard to faith that first it is laid on a sure foundation.

14. For Abel, because of his faith his offering was accepted. And Enoch, because he was well-pleasing through his faith, was removed from death. Noah, because he believed, was preserved from the deluge. Abraham, through his faith, obtained blessing, and it was accounted to him for righteousness. Isaac, because he believed, was loved. Jacob, because of his faith, was preserved. Joseph, because of his faith, was tried in the waters of contention, and was delivered from his trial, and his Lord established a witness in him, as David said:—Witness hath he established in Joseph. Moses also by his faith performed many wonderful works of power. By his faith he destroyed the Egyptians with ten plagues. Again, by faith he divided the sea, and caused his people to cross over and sank the Egyptians in the midst of it. By faith he cast the wood into the bitter waters and they became sweet. By faith he brought down manna and satisfied his people. By faith he spread out his hands and conquered Amalek, as is written:—His hands continued in faith till the setting of the sun. Also by faith he went up to Mount Sinai, when he twice fasted for the space of forty days. Again by faith he conquered Sihon and Og, the Kings of the Amorites.

15. This is wonderful, my beloved, and a great prodigy that Moses did in the Red Sea, when the waters were divided by faith, and stood up on high like mountains or like mighty cliffs. They were checked and stood still at the commandment; they were closed up as in vessels, and fast bound in the height as in the depth. Their fluidity did not overflow the boundary, but rather they changed the nature of their creation. Irrational creatures became obedient. The billows became rigid and were awaiting the vengeance, when the people should have passed over. Wonderful was it how the waves stood still and expected the commandment and the vengeance. The foundations (hidden) from the ages of the world were revealed, and that which from the beginning had been liquid suddenly became dry. The gates lifted up their heads and the everlasting gates were lifted up. The pillar of fire entered and illuminated the entire camp. The

people passed over by faith. And the judgment of righteousness was wrought upon Pharaoh and upon his host and upon his chariots.

16. Thus also Joshua the son of Nun divided Jordan by his faith, and the children of Israel crossed over as in the days of Moses. But know, my beloved, that this passage of the Jordan was three times laid open by its being divided. First through Joshua the Son of Nun, and secondly through Elijah, and then through Elisha. For the word of the Book makes known that over against this passage of Jericho, there Elijah was taken up to heaven; for when Elisha turned back from following him and divided the Jordan and passed over, the children of the Prophets of Jericho came out to meet Elisha and said:—The spirit of Elijah rests upon Elisha. Furthermore when the people crossed over in the days of Joshua the son of Nun (it was there), for thus it is written:—The people passed over, over against Jericho. Also Joshua the son of Nun by faith cast down the walls of Jericho, and they fell without difficulty. Again by faith he destroyed thirty-one kings and made the children of Israel to inherit the land. Furthermore by his faith he spread out his hands towards heaven and stayed the sun in Gibeon and the moon in the valley of Ajalon. And they were stayed and stood still from their courses. But enough! All the righteous, our fathers, in all that they did were victorious through faith, as also the blessed Apostle testified with regard to all of them:—By faith they prevailed. Again Solomon said:—Many men are called merciful, but a faithful man who can find? Also Job thus said:—My integrity, shall not pass from me, and in my righteousness will persist.

17. Also our Saviour used thus to say to every one who drew near to Him to be healed:—According to thy faith be unto thee. And when the blind man approached Him, He said to him:—Dost thou believe that I am able to heal thee? That blind man said to Him:—Yea, Lord, I believe. And his faith opened his eyes. And to him whose son was sick, He said:—Believe and thy son shall live. He said to Him:—I believe, Lord; help thou my feeble faith. And by his faith his son was healed. And also when the nobleman came near to Him, by his faith was his boy healed, when he said to our Lord:—Speak the word and my servant will be cured. And our Lord was astonished at his faith, and according to his faith it happened to him. And also when the chief of the Synagogue requested Him concerning his daughter, He said thus to him:—Only firmly believe and thy daughter shall live. So he believed and his daughter lived and arose. And when Lazarus died, our Lord said to Martha:—If thou believest, thy brother shall rise. Martha saith unto Him;—Yea, Lord, I believe. And He raised him after four days. And also Simon who was called Cephas because of his faith was called the firm rock. And again when our Lord gave the Sacra-

ment of Baptism to His apostles, He said thus to them:—Whosoever believeth and is baptized shall live, and whosoever believeth not shall be condemned. Again He said to his Apostles:—If ye believe and doubt not, there is nothing ye shall not be able to do. For when our Lord walked on the billows of the sea, Simon also by his faith walked with Him; but when in respect of his faith he doubted, and began to sink, our Lord called him, thou of little faith. And when the Apostles asked of our Lord, they begged nothing at His hands but this, saying to Him:—Increase our faith. He said to them:—If there were in you faith, even a mountain would remove from before you. And He said to them:—Doubt ye not, lest ye sink down in the midst of the world, even as Simon when he doubted began to sink in the midst of the sea. And again He said thus;—This shall be the sign for those that believe; they shall speak with new tongues and shall cast out demons, and they shall lay their hands on the sick and they shall be made whole.

18. Let us draw near then, my beloved, to faith, since its powers are so many. For faith raised up to the heavens (Enoch), and conquered the Deluge. It caused the barren to bring forth. It delivered from the sword. It raised up from the pit. It enriched the poor. It released the captives. It delivered the persecuted. It brought down the fire. It divided the sea. It cleft the rock, and gave to the thirsty water to drink. It satisfied the hungry. It raised the dead, and brought them up from Sheol. It stilled the billows. It healed the sick. It conquered hosts. It overthrew walls. It stopped the mouths of lions, and quenched the flame of fire. It humiliated the proud, and brought the humble to honour. All these mighty works were wrought by faith.

19. Now thus is faith; when a man believes in God the Lord of all, Who made the heavens and the earth and the seas and all that is in them; and He made Adam in His image; and He gave the Law to Moses; He sent of His Spirit upon the prophets; He sent moreover His Christ into the world. Furthermore that a man should believe in the resurrection of the dead; and should furthermore also believe in the sacrament of baptism. This is the faith of the Church of God. And (it is necessary) that a man should separate himself from the observance of hours and Sabbaths and moons and seasons, and divinations and sorceries and Chaldaean arts and magic, from fornication and from festive music, from vain doctrines, which are instruments of the Evil One, from the blandishment of honeyed words, from blasphemy and from adultery. And that a man should not bear false witness, and that a man should not speak with double tongue. These then are the works of the faith which is based on the true Stone which is Christ, on Whom the whole building is reared up.

20. Furthermore, my beloved, there is much besides in the Holy Books about faith. But these few things out of the much have I written to recall them to thy love that thou mayest know and make known and believe and also be believed. And when thou hast read and learned the works of faith, thou mayest be made like unto that tilled land upon which the good seed fell, and produced fruit a hundred-fold and sixty-fold and thirty-fold. And when thou comest to thy Lord, He may call thee a good servant and prudent and faithful, who on account of His faith, that abounded, is to enter into the Kingdom of his Lord.

Demonstration V

Of Wars

1. This reflection has befallen me at this time concerning the shaking that is to take place at this time, and the host that has assembled itself for the sword. The times were disposed beforehand by God. The times of peace are fulfilled in the days of the good and just; and the times of many evils are fulfilled in the days of the evil and transgressors. For it is thus written:—Good must happen and blessed is he through whom it shall come to pass; and evil must happen, but woe to him through whom it shall come to pass. Good has come to the people of God, and blessedness awaits that man through whom the good came. And evil is stirred up as regards the host that is gathered together by means of the evil and arrogant one who glories; and woe also is there reserved for him through whom the evil is stirred up. But do not, my beloved, reproach the evil person who has inflicted evil upon many; because the times were beforehand disposed and the time of their accomplishment has arrived.

2. Therefore because it is the time of the Evil One, hear in mystery that which I am writing for thee. For thus it is written:—Whatsoever is exalted amongst men is despicable before God. And again it is written:—Everyone who exalteth himself shall be abased, and everyone who humbleth himself shall be exalted. Also Jeremiah said:—Let not the mighty glory in his might, nor the rich in his riches. And again the blessed Apostle said:—Whosoever glorieth, let him glory in the Lord. And David said:—I saw the wicked exalted and lifted up as the cedar of Lebanon; and when I passed by he was not, and I sought him and found him not.

3. For every one that glories shall be humbled. Cain gloried over Abel his brother and slew him. And he was cursed and became a fugitive and a vagabond in the earth. Again the Sodomites gloried over Lot, and there fell upon them fire from heaven and burned them up and their city was overthrown upon them. And Esau gloried over Jacob and persecuted him, and Jacob

received the birthright and blessings of Esau. And the children of Jacob gloried over Joseph, and (afterwards) fell down and worshipped him in Egypt. And Pharaoh gloried over Moses and over his people; and Pharaoh and his host were drowned in the sea. And Dathan and Abiram gloried over Moses, and they went down alive to Sheol. And Goliath threatened David, and he fell before him and was crushed. And again Saul persecuted David, and he fell by the sword of the Philistines. And Absalom exalted himself against him, and Joab slew him in the battle. Again Benhadad gloried over Ahab, and he was delivered into the hand of Israel. And Sennacherib blasphemed against Hezekiah and his God, and his host became dead carcases when one of the Watchers went forth and slew in the camp one hundred and eighty-five thousand at the prayer of Hezekiah and at the prayer of Prophet Isaiah, most glorious of the Prophets. Ahab exalted himself over Micah, and he went up and fell in Ramoth Gilead. Jezebel gloried over Elijah, and the dogs devoured her in the portion of Jezreel. Haman gloried over Mordecai, and his iniquity turned back upon his own head. The Babylonians gloried over Daniel and cast him into the den of lions, and Daniel came up victorious, and they were cast instead of him into the den. Again the Babylonians gloried and accused Hananiah and his companions, and they were cast into the furnace of fire; and they came up victorious and the flame devoured the accusers.

4. Now Nebuchadnezzar said:—I will ascend to heaven and exalt my throne above the stars of God and sit in the lofty mountains that are in the borders of the North. Isaiah said concerning him:—Because thy heart has thus exalted thee, therefore thou shalt be brought down to Sheol, and all that look upon thee shall be astonished at thee. And Sennacherib also said thus:—I will go up to the summit of the mountains and to the shoulders of Lebanon. I will dig and drink water and will dry up with my horses' hoofs all the deep rivers. And because he thus exalted himself, Isaiah again said concerning him:—Why does the axe boast itself against him that cutteth with it, or the saw exalt itself against him that saweth with it, or the rod lift itself up against him that wieldeth it? For thou, Sennacherib, art the axe in the hands of Him that cuts, and thou art the saw in the hands of Him that saws, and the rod in the hand of Him that wields thee for chastisement, and thou art the staff for smiting. Thou art sent against the fickle people, and again thou art ordained against the stubborn people, that thou mayest carry away the captivity and take the spoil; and thou hast made them as the mire of the streets for all men and for all the Gentiles. And when thou hast done all these things, why art thou exalted against Him Who holds thee, and why dost thou boast against Him Who saws with thee, and why hast thou reviled the holy city? and hast said to the chil-

dren of Jerusalem:—Can your God deliver you from my hand? And thou hast dared to say:—Who is the Lord that He shall deliver you from my hands? Because of this, hear the word of the Lord, saying:—I will crush the Assyrian in My land, and on My mountains will I tread him down. And when he shall have been crushed and trodden down, the Virgin, the daughter of Zion, will despise him, and the daughter of Jerusalem will shake her head and say:—Whom hast thou reviled and blasphemed, and against whom hast thou lifted up thy voice? Thou hast lifted up thine eyes towards heaven against the Holy One of Israel, and by the hands of thy messengers thou hast reviled the Lord. Now see that the hook has been forced into thy nostrils, and the bridle into thy lips, and thou hast turned back with thine heart crushed, who camest with thine heart uplifted. And his slaying was by the hands of his loved ones; and in the house of his confidence, there was he overthrown, and fell before his god. And truly it was right, my beloved, that his body should thus become a sacrifice and offering before that god on whom he relied, and in his temple, as a memorial for his idol.

5. Again the ram was lifted up and exalted, and pushed with its horns towards the west, and towards the north, and towards the south, and humbled many beasts. And they could not stand before him, until the he-goat came from the west and smote the ram and broke his horns and humbled the ram completely. But the ram was the King of Media and Persia, that is, Darius; and the he-goat was Alexander, the son of Philip, the Macedonian. For Daniel saw the ram when he was in the East before the gate of Shushan the fortress that is in the province of Elam, upon the river Ulai. And he was pushing towards the West and towards the North and towards the South. And none of the beasts could stand before him. And the he-goat of the goats came up from the region of the Greeks, and exalted himself against the ram. And he smote him and broke both his horns, the greater and the lesser. And why did he say that he broke both his horns? Clearly because he humbled both the kingdoms which he ruled; the lesser, that of the Medes, and the greater, that of the Persians. But when Alexander the Greek came, he slew Darius, King of Media and Persia. For thus the angel said to Daniel, when he was explaining the vision to him:—The ram that thou sawest was the King of Media and Persia, and the he-goat the King of the Greeks. Now, from the time that the two horns of the ram were broken, until this time, there have been six hundred and forty-eight years.

6. Therefore, as for the ram, its horns are broken. And though its horns are broken, lo! it exalts and uplifts itself against the fourth beast, that is strong and mighty and its teeth of iron and its hoofs of brass, and it shall devour and grind down, and trample with its feet whatsoever remaineth. O Ram, whose

horns are broken, rest thou from the beast, and provoke it not lest it devour thee and grind thee to powder. The ram could not stand before the he-goat; how shall it stand before that terrible beast, whose mouth speaketh great things, and whatsoever it finds it couches over as a lion over his prey? Whoever provokes the lion becomes its portion; and whoever stirs up that beast, it shall devour him. And who is there that shall escape out from under the feet of that beast when it is trampling on him? For the beast shall not be slain until the Ancient of Days shall sit upon the throne, and the Son of Man shall come near before Him, and authority shall be given to Him. Then shall that beast be slain and its carcase shall perish. And the Kingdom of the Son of Man shall be established, an eternal Kingdom, and His authority from generation to generation.

7. Be quiet, O thou that dost exalt thyself; vaunt not thyself! For if thy wealth has lifted up thy heart, it is not more abundant than that of Hezekiah, who went in and boasted of it before the Babylonians, (yet) it was all of it carried away and went to Babylon. And if thou gloriest in thy children, they shall be led away from thee to the Beast, as the children of King Hezekiah were led away, and became eunuchs in the palace of the King of Babylon. And if thou dost glory in thy wisdom, thou dost not in it excel the Prince of Tyre, whom Ezekiel reproached, saying unto him:—Art thou wiser than Daniel, or hast thou seen by thy wisdom the things that are hid? And if thy mind is puffed up by thy years, that they are many; they are not more in number than those of the Prince of Tyre who ruled the Kingdom during the days of twenty-two Kings of the house of Judah, that is, for four hundred and forty years. And since the years of that King of Tyre were many, all the time he thus said in his heart, I am God and sit in the seat of God in the heart of the seas. But Ezekiel said to him: Thou art a man and thou art not God. For while the Prince of Tyre was walking without fault in the midst of the stones of fire, there was mercy upon him. But when his heart was lifted up, the cherub who overshadoweth, destroyed him.

8. Now, what are the stones of fire, but the children of Zion and the children of Jerusalem? For in the ancient time, in the days of David and of Solomon his son, Hiram was a friend to those of the house of Israel. But when they were carried away captive from their place, he rejoiced over them and spurned them with his feet, and did not remember the friendship of the house of David. And as to that which I said that the children of Judah were called the stones of fire, it was not of my own thought that I said it, but Jeremiah the Prophet spake concerning them; for when he was calling forth tears for them in the Lamentations, he said:—The children of Zion were more excellent than

precious stones. And again he said:—How are the stones of the Sanctuary cast down at the head of all the streets? And again He said by the Prophet:—The stones were holy that were cast down in his land. And as to these very stones, the fire was burning in them, as Jeremiah said:—The word of the Lord became in my heart like burning fire and it was hot in my bones. And again He said to Jeremiah:—Lo! I give My word in thy mouth as fire, and this people shall be as wood. And again He said words shall go forth as fire, and as iron that cutteth the stone. On this account the Prophets, amongst whom Hiram the Prince of Tyre was walking, were called stones of fire.

9. And again (God) said to him:—Thou wast with the Cherub who was anointed and overshadowing. For the king, who was anointed with the holy oil, was called a Cherub. And he was overshadowing all his people, as Jeremiah said:—The anointed of the Lord is the breath of our nostrils, he of whom we said that in his shadow shall we live amongst the Gentiles. For they were sitting in the shadow of the king, while he was standing at their head. And when the crown of their head fell, they were without shade. And if any one should say that this word is spoken concerning Christ, let him receive that which I write for him without disputation, and thus he will be persuaded that it was said with reference to the king. For Jeremiah said in behalf of the people:—Woe unto us, for the crown of our head has fallen! But Christ has not fallen, because He rose again the third day. For the king fell from the house of Judah, and never again was their kingdom set up. And as for that He said again:—I will destroy the overshadowing Cherub. For the Cherub that He will destroy is Nebuchadnezzar, as it is written:—He performed a work in Tyre, and there was given him by Tyre no hire for his host, and in return for the work of Tyre there was given him the land of Egypt. And why was hire not given by Tyre to Nebuchadnezzar? Clearly because its wealth went away in the sea, so that Nebuchadnezzar did not receive it. And at that time He destroyed the overshadowing Cherub, which is Nebuchadnezzar. For there are two Cherubs, one anointed and overshadowing, and one overshadowing but not anointed. For He said above:—Thou wast with the Cherub anointed and overshadowing. And lower down He said:—I will destroy thee the overshadowing Cherub; and did not say "anointed." For Nebuchadnezzar was not anointed; but David and Solomon were, and the other kings who arose after them. And how was Nebuchadnezzar called overshadowing? Clearly on account of the vision of the tree, when he saw a tree in the midst of the earth, beneath which dwelt all the beasts of the wilderness and on its branches dwelt all the birds of heaven, and from it all flesh was fed. When Daniel interpreted his dream to him, Daniel said to him:—Thou art the tree, that tree which thou

sawest in the midst of the earth and beneath thee dwell all the nations. On this account he was the overshadowing Cherub; who destroyed the Prince of Tyre, because he rejoiced over the children of Israel, for that they were carried away captive from their land, and because his heart was exalted. This Tyre also lay waste seventy years like Jerusalem which sat in desolation seventy years. For Isaiah said concerning it:—Tyre shall wander seventy years, as the days of one king, and shall commit fornication with all the kingdoms that are upon the face of the earth.

10. O thou that art exalted and lifted up, let not the vaunting of thine heart mislead thee, nor say thou, I will go up against the rich land and against the powerful beast. For that beast will not be slain by the ram seeing that its horns are broken. For the he-goat broke the horns of the ram. Now the he-goat has become the mighty beast. For when the children of Japhet held the kingdom, then they slew Darius, the king of Persia. Now the fourth beast has swallowed up the third. And this third consists of the children of Japhet, and the fourth consists of the children of Shem, for they are the children of Esau. Because, when Daniel saw the vision of the four beasts, he saw first the children of Ham, the seed of Nimrod, which the Babylonians are; and secondly, the Persians and Medes, who are the children of Japhet; and thirdly, the Greeks, the brethren of the Medes; and fourthly, the children of Shem, which the children of Esau are. For a confederacy was formed between the children of Japhet and the children of Shem. Then the government was taken away from the children of Japhet, the younger, and was given to Shem, the elder; and to this day it continues, and will continue for ever. But when the time of the consummation of the dominion of the children of Shem shall have come, the Ruler, who came forth from the children of Judah, shall receive the kingdom, when He shall come in His second Advent.

11. For in the vision of Nebuchadnezzar, when he saw it, which Daniel made known and showed to Nebuchadnezzar, when he saw the image which stood over against him, the head of the image was of gold, and its breast and arms of silver, and its belly and thighs of brass, and its legs and feet of iron and potter's clay. And Daniel said to Nebuchadnezzar:—Thou art the head of gold. And why was he called the head of gold? Was it not because the word of Jeremiah was fulfilled in him? For Jeremiah said:—Babylon is a golden cup in the hand of the Lord, that makes all the earth to drink of its wine. And also Babylon was called the head of all the kingdoms, as it is written:—Babylon was the head of the of Nimrod.

12. And he said that the breast and the arms of the image were of silver. This signified concerning a kingdom which was inferior to it; namely, Darius

the Mede. For (God) put the kingdom into the balance. For the kingdom of the house of Nimrod was weighed and was found wanting. And since it was wanting, Darius received it. Because of this he said that his kingdom was inferior. And because it was inferior, the children of Media did not rule in all the earth. Now the belly and thighs of the image were of brass, and he said:—The third kingdom shall rule in all the earth. It is the kingdom of the children of Javan, who are children of Japhet. For the children of Javan came in against the kingdom of their brethren. For Madai and Javan are sons of Japhet. But Madai was foolish and incapable of governing the kingdom, until Javan, his brother came, who was wise and cunning, to destroy the kingdom. For Alexander, son of Philip, ruled in all the earth.

13. And the legs and feet of the image were of iron. This is the kingdom of the children of Shem, who are the children of Esau, which is strong as iron. And he said:—As iron breaks and subdueth everything, so also the fourth kingdom shall break and bruise everything. And he explained with reference to the feet and toes, that part of them was of iron and part of them of potter's clay. For he said:—Thus they shall be mingled with the seed of man, and they shall not cleave one to another, as iron cannot be mixed with clay. This referred to the fourth kingdom. Because in the kingdom of the children of Esau there was not a king, the son of a king, established to govern the kingdom; but when the children of Esau were gathered together into a powerful city, then they made a senate. And from thence they used to set up as chief of the city a wise man to govern the kingdom, lest when the Governor of their kingdom should weigh them, they might be found wanting, and the kingdom might be taken away from them as the kingdom of the children of arrogant Nimrod was taken away and given to the children of foolish Madai. And this king who was set up, the seed of that former king was destroying him; and they did not cleave one to another. But as to the seed of man which is compared with the clay, the meaning is this; that when the king was chosen for the kingdom, he mingled himself with the root of the kingdom of iron.

14. And he showed that in the days of those kings, who shall arise in the kingdom, the God of heaven will set up a kingdom which shall not be destroyed and shall not pass away for ever. This is the Kingdom of King Messiah, which is that which shall cause the fourth kingdom to pass away. And above he said:—Thou sawest a stone which was cut out, but not by hands; and it smote the image upon its feet of iron and potter's clay and broke them to pieces. Now he did not say that it smote upon the head of the image, nor on its breast and arms, nor yet on its belly and thighs, but on its feet; because that, of the whole image, that stone when it comes will find the feet alone. And in the next

verse he said:—The iron and the brass and the silver and the gold were broken to pieces together. For after them, when King Messiah shall reign, then He will humble the fourth kingdom, and will break the whole image; for by the whole image the world is meant. Its head is Nebuchadnezzar; its breast and arms the King of Media and Persia; its belly and thighs the King of the Greeks; its legs and feet the kingdom of the children of Esau; the stone, which smote the image and brake it, and with which the whole earth was filled, is the kingdom of King Messiah, Who will bring to nought the kingdom of this world, and He will rule for ever and ever.

15. Again hear concerning the vision of the four beasts which Daniel saw coming up out of the sea and diverse one from another. This is the appearance of them:—The first was like a lion, and it had the wings of an eagle. And I saw that its wings were plucked away, and it stood up like a man upon its feet, and the heart of a man was given to it. And the second beast was like a bear, and it raised itself up upon one side and there were three ribs in its mouth between its teeth. And the third beast was like a leopard, and it had four wings and four heads. And the fourth beast was exceedingly terrible and strong and powerful, and it had great teeth. It devoured and brake to pieces, and whatsoever remained, it stamped with its feet. Now the great sea that Daniel saw is the world: and these four beasts are the four kingdoms signified above.

16. Now as to the first beast, he said concerning it, that it was like a lion, and it had the wings of an eagle. For the first beast was the kingdom of Babylon, which was like a lion. For thus Jeremiah wrote saying:—Israel is a wandering sheep. The lions caused them to wander. First the king of Assyria devoured him. And this last was stronger than he, Nebuchadnezzar king of Babylon. So Jeremiah called him a lion. And he said:—He has the wings of an eagle. For thus it is written that, when Nebuchadnezzar went out to the wilderness with the beasts, he grew hair like (the plumage) of an eagle. And he said:—I saw that its wings were plucked away and it stood upright upon its feet as a man, and a man's heart was given to it. For first, in the vision of the image, he was compared to gold which is more precious than anything which is used in the world. So in the vision of the beasts he is compared to a lion which excels in its might all the beasts. And again he was compared to an eagle which surpasses every bird. Whatsoever was written about him was fulfilled in him. For the Lord said concerning him:—I have placed a yoke of iron upon the neck of all the nations, and they shall serve the king of Babylon seventy years. And also the beasts of the desert and the birds of heaven have I given to him to serve him. For since the king was like the head of gold, men served him as a king. And when he went out to the wilderness, the beasts served him as a lion. And

when his hair was like (the plumage) of an eagle, the birds of heaven served him as an eagle. But when his heart was lifted up, and he knew not that the power was given to him from heaven, the yoke of iron was broken from the neck of men, and he went forth with the beasts, and instead of the heart of a king there was given him the heart of a lion. And when he was lifted up over the beasts, the heart of a lion was taken away from him, and there was given him the heart of a bird. And when wings grew upon him like those of an eagle, he exalted himself over the birds. And then his wings also were plucked away and there was given to him a humble heart. And when he knew that the Most High has authority in the kingdom of man, to give it to whomsoever He will, then as a man he praised Him.

17. And as for the second beast, he said concerning him that it was like a bear and raised itself up upon one side. Because when the kingdom of Media and Persia arose, it arose in the east. And three ribs were in its mouth. Because the ram was pushing towards the West and towards the North and towards the South, towards three winds of heaven. These three winds it held, and pushed against, like the three ribs that were in the mouth of the bear; until the he-goat came forth from the west, and smote the ram and took out the ribs that were in his mouth.

18. And concerning the third beast he said that it was like a leopard, and it had four birds' wings on its back and that beast had four heads. Now this third beast was Alexander the Macedonian. For he was strong as a leopard. And as for the four wings and the four heads that the beast had, that was because he gave the kingdom to his four friends to govern after him, when he had come and slain Darius and reigned in his stead.

19. And of the fourth beast he said that it was exceedingly terrible and strong and mighty, devouring and crushing and trampling with its feet anything that remained. It is the kingdom of the children of Esau. Because after that Alexander the Macedonian became king, the kingdom of the Greeks was founded, since Alexander also was one of them, even of the Greeks. But the vision of the third beast was fulfilled in him, since the third and the fourth were one. Now Alexander reigned for twelve years. And the kings of the Greeks arose after Alexander, being seventeen kings, and their years were two hundred and sixty-nine years from Seleucus Nicanor to Ptolemy. And the Caesars were from Augustus to Philip Caesar, seventeen kings. And their years are two hundred and ninety-three years; and eighteen years of Severus.

20. For Daniel said:—I was considering the ten horns that were upon the head of the beast. For the ten horns were ten kings who arose at that time until Antiochus. And he said:—A little horn arose from between those ten and three

fell before it. For when Antiochus arose in the kingdom, he humbled three kings, and he exalted himself against the saints of the Most High and against Jerusalem. And he defiled the sanctuary. And he caused the sacrifice and the offerings to cease for a week and half a week, namely, for ten and a-half years. And he brought in fornicators into the house of the Lord, and he caused the observances of the Law to cease. And he slew righteous men and gave them to the birds of heaven and to the beasts of the earth. For in his days was fulfilled the word that David spoke:—O God, the Gentiles have come into thine inheritance, and have defiled Thy holy temple. They have made Jerusalem desolate. They have given the dead bodies of Thy servants as food to the birds of heaven, and the flesh of Thy righteous ones to the beasts of the earth. They have poured out their blood like water round about Jerusalem, and there is none to bury them. For this was accomplished at that time, when the venerable and aged Eleazar was slain, and the sons of the blessed Samuna, seven in number, and when Judas (Maccabeus) and his brethren were struggling on behalf of their people, when they were dwelling in hiding-places. At that time the horn made war with the saints, and their power prevailed. And the wicked Antiochus spake words against the Most High, and changed the times and the seasons. And he made to cease the covenant of Abraham, and abolished the Sabbath of rest. For he commanded the Jews that they should not circumcise. Therefore, (the Prophet) said concerning him;—He shall think to change the times and the seasons and the laws, and they were given into his hand for a time, times, and half a time. Now the time and half a time is the week and a half, which is ten years and a half. Again he said:—The judgment was set and they took away his authority from him, to injure and destroy him until the end of the kingdom. For the judgment came upon Antiochus, a judgment from heaven; and he became sick with a grievous and evil sickness, and on account of the smell of him as he rotted, no man could approach him, for worms were crawling and falling from him and eating his flesh because he oppressed the worm Jacob. And his flesh rotted in his lifetime, because he caused the dead bodies of the sons of Jerusalem to rot and they were not buried. And he became defiled in his own eyes, because he had defiled the sanctuary of God. And he prayed and was not heard, because he did not hearken to the groanings of the righteous whom he slew. For he wrote a letter and sent it to the Jews and called them "my friends," but God had not mercy on him, but he died in his torment.

21. He said again:—The saints of the Most High shall receive the Kingdom. What shall we say concerning this? Have the children of Israel received the Kingdom of the Most High? God forbid. Or has that people come upon

the clouds of heaven? This has passed away from them. For Jeremiah said concerning them:—Call them rejected silver, for the Lord has rejected them. Again he said:—He will not again regard them. And Isaiah said concerning them:—Pass by; pass by; approach not the defiled. And concerning the saints of the Most High (Daniel) said thus:—They shall inherit the Kingdom for ever. For these rested a little from the burden of kings and princes, namely, from after the death of Antiochus till the sixty-two weeks were fulfilled. And the Son of Man came to free them and gather them together, but they did not receive Him. For He came to obtain fruit from them, and they did not give it to Him. For their vines were of the vine of Sodom and of the stock of Gomorrha, a vineyard in which thorns grew, and which bore wild grapes. Their vine was bitter, and their fruit sour. The thorns could not be softened, nor could the bitterness change to the nature of wine, nor could the sour fruit change to a sweet nature.

22. For Isaiah first set men of Judah as judges over them, and there was planted amongst them a new and beloved planting. But these are those judges who shall sit on twelve thrones and judge their twelve tribes. And thus He said to the judges:—Judge between Me and My vineyard, what further, O ye judges, should I have done to My vineyard, that I did not do? For lo! I planted it with vine scions, and they became strange vines. I surrounded it with a fence of heavenly Watchers and I built its tower, the holy Temple. And I dug out its winepress, the baptism of the priests. And I brought down rain upon it, the words of My Prophets. And I pruned it and trimmed it, from the works of the Amorites. I looked that it should produce grapes of righteousness, and it produced wild grapes of iniquity and sin. I looked for judgment and behold oppression, and for righteousness and there was a cry. Hear, O ye judges, what I will do to My vineyard. I will break open its fence, and it shall be for downtreading. And I will tear down its tower, and it shall be for pillage. And I will make it to become a desert because it produced wild grapes. And it shall not be dressed and it shall not be pruned. And thorns and weeds shall grow up in it. And I will command the clouds that they send not down rain upon it. For the heavenly Watchers departed from the fence of the vineyard; and the mighty tower on which they relied was torn down. The winepress, the cleansing away of their offences, was overthrown. When the vine was without blemish, it did not prove of service. Now that the fire has devoured it and that it is laid waste, how shall it prove of service? The fire has devoured its two branches and its inward parts are wasted. For its two branches are the two kingdoms, and its inward part which is laid waste is Jerusalem. Many servants were sent to them by the Lord of the vineyard. And they slew them and did not send the fruit to

the Lord of the vineyard. After the servants the beloved Son was sent, to receive from them the fruit and to bring it back to Him that sent Him. And they seized Him and cast Him out of the vineyard; and they cut spikes from the thorns of the vineyard and fixed them in His hands. And He was hungry and asked food of them; and they took and gave Him gall from the fruit of the vineyard. He was thirsty and asked of them drink; and they gave Him vinegar and He would not drink it. And they platted a crown of thorns that had sprung up in the vineyard, and placed it on the head of the Son of the Lord of the vineyard. For from the time that the vineyard was made, it displayed these fruits. Therefore its Lord uprooted it and cast it in the fire; and planted good fruit-bearing vines in the vineyard, and such as gladden the husbandman. For Christ is the vineyard, and His Father is the husbandman; and they who drink of His cup are the vines. Therefore vineyard was formed instead of vineyard. And furthermore at His coming He handed over the kingdom to the Romans, as the children of Esau are called. And these children of Esau will keep the kingdom for its giver.

23. And the holy People inherited an eternal Kingdom; the holy people who were chosen instead of the People. For He provoked them to jealousy with a people that was not a people. And with a foolish people He angered them. And He set free the holy people. For lo! every covenant of God is freed from the burden of kings and princes. For even if a man has served the heathen, as soon as ever he draws nigh unto the covenant of God, he is set free. But the Jews are toiling in bondage amongst the Gentiles. For thus he said about the Saints;—They shall inherit the Kingdom that is beneath the heaven. But if he had said it about them (the Jews), why are they toiling in service amongst the Gentiles? And if they say that it has not taken place as yet; then (we ask) is the Kingdom that shall be given to the Son of man, to be heavenly or earthly? And lo! the children of the Kingdom are sealed, and they have received their emancipation from this world. For since it exists now, it will not be willing to be subjected to the power of the King, Who shall come and take to Himself His Kingdom. But it will guard His pledges with honour, that when He shall come to bring to nought the Kingdom, he may come upon them not in anger. For when He, Whose is the Kingdom, shall come in His second coming, He will take to Himself whatever He has given. And He Himself will be King for ever and ever. And His Kingdom shall not pass away, because it is an eternal Kingdom.

24. For first, He gave the Kingdom to the sons of Jacob, and subdued to them the children of Esau; as Isaac said to Esau:—Thou shalt serve Jacob thy brother. And when again they did not prosper in the Kingdom, He took it

away from the children of Jacob and gave it to the children of Esau until He should come Whose it is. And they will deliver up the deposit to its Giver, and will not deal fraudulently with it. And the Guardian of the Kingdom is subject to Him to Whom all things are subject. Therefore this Kingdom of the children of Esau shall not be delivered up into the hand of the hosts that are gathered together, that desire to go up against it; because the Kingdom is being kept safe for its Giver, and He Himself will preserve it. And as to this that I wrote to thee, beloved, that the Kingdom of the children of Esau is being kept safe for its Giver, doubt not about it, that that Kingdom will not be conquered. For a mighty champion Whose name is Jesus shall come with power, and bearing as His armour all the power of the Kingdom. And search out and see that also by the poll-tax He was enrolled amongst them. And as He was enrolled by the poll-tax amongst them, He will also succour them. And His standard abounds in that place, and they are clothed in His armour, and shall not be found wanting in war. And if thou shouldest say unto me:—"In the years of the Kings that preceded these, why did they conquer and subdue the beast?" It was because the chiefs and kings who stood up at that time in the Kingdom of the children of Esau did not wish to lead with them to the war the Man who was enrolled with them in the poll-tax. Therefore the beast was subdued a little, but was not slain.

25. But concerning these things that I have written for thee, my beloved, namely, concerning that which is written in Daniel, I have not brought them to an end, but (have stopped) short of the end. And if any man dispute about them, say thus to him, that these words are not concluded, because the words of God are infinite, nor will they be concluded. For the foolish man says, "Here unto (these) words reach." And again, it is not possible to add to them or to diminish from them. For the riches of God cannot be computed or limited. For if thou take away water from the sea, the deficiency will be imperceptible. And if thou remove sand from the sea-shore, its measure will not be diminished. And if thou count the stars of heaven, thou wilt not arrive at the sum of them. And if thou kindle fire from a burning, it will not a whit be lessened. And if thou receive of the Spirit of Christ, Christ will not a whit be diminished. And if Christ dwell in thee, yet He will not be completed in thee. And if the sun enter the windows of thy house, yet the sun in its entirety will not come to thee. And all these things that I have enumerated for thee were created by the word of God. Therefore know thou, that, as concerning the word of God no man has reached or will reach its end. Therefore, have thou no disputation about these things, but say:—"These things are so. That is enough." But hear these things from me, and also enquire about them of our

brethren, children of our faith. But whosoever shall mock at the words of his brother, even if he say, "mine are wise," yet hearken not to his words. And concerning what I wrote to thee about these forces that are being stirred up to war, it is not as though anything has been revealed to me that I have made known these things to thee, but attend to the words at the head of the letter:—Every one who exalteth himself shall be humbled. For even if the forces shall go up and conquer, yet know that it is a chastisement of God; and though they conquer, they shall be condemned in a righteous judgment. But yet be thou assured of this, that the beast shall be slain at its (appointed) time. But do thou, my brother, at this time be earnest in imploring mercy, that there may be peace upon the people of God.

Demonstration VI

Of Monks

1. Expedient is the word that I speak and worthy of acceptance:—Let us now awake from our sleep, and lift up both our hearts and hands to God towards heaven; lest suddenly the Lord of the house come, that when He comes He may find us in watchfulness. Let us observe the appointed time of the glorious bridegroom, that we may enter with Him into His bride-chamber. Let us prepare oil for our lamps that we may go forth to meet Him with joy. Let us make ready provision for our abiding-place, for the way that is narrow and strait. And let us put away and cast from us all uncleanness, and put on wedding garments. Let us trade with the silver that we have received, that we may be called diligent servants. Let us be constant in prayer, that we may pass by the place where fear dwells. Let us cleanse our heart from iniquity, that we may see the Lofty One in His honour. Let us be merciful, as it is written, that God may have mercy upon us. Let there be peace amongst us, that we may be called the brethren of Christ. Let us hunger for righteousness, that we may be satisfied from the table of His Kingdom. Let us be the salt of truth, that we may not become food for the serpent. Let us purge our seed from thorns, that we may produce fruit a hundred-fold. Let us found our building on the rock, that it may not be shaken by the winds and waves. Let us be vessels unto honour that we may be required by the Lord for His use. Let us sell all our possessions, and buy for ourselves the pearl, that we may be rich. Let us lay up our treasures in heaven, that when we come we may open them and have pleasure in them. Let us visit our Lord in the persons of the sick, that He may invite us to stand at His right hand. Let us hate ourselves and love Christ, as He loved us and gave Himself up for our sakes. Let us honour the spirit of Christ, that we may receive grace from Him. Let us be strangers to the world, even as Christ was not of it. Let us be humble and mild, that we may inherit the land of life. Let us be unflagging in His service, that He may cause us to serve in the abode of

the saints. Let us pray His prayer in purity, that it may have access to the Lord of Majesty. Let us be partakers in His suffering, that so we may also rise up in His resurrection. Let us bear His sign upon our bodies, that we may be delivered from the wrath to come. For fearful is the day in which He will come, and who is able to endure it? Furious and hot is His wrath, and it will destroy all the wicked. Let us set upon our head the helmet of redemption, that we may not be wounded and die in the battle. Let us gird our loins with truth, that we may not be found impotent in the contest. Let us arise and awaken Christ, that He may still the stormy blasts from us. Let us take as a shield against the Evil One, the preparation of the Gospel of our Redeemer. Let us receive power from our Lord to tread upon snakes and scorpions. Let us lay aside from us wrath, with all fury and malice. Let no reviling proceed out of our mouth, with which we pray unto God. Let us not be cursers, that we may be delivered from the curse of the law. Let us be diligent workers, that we may obtain our reward with those of old. Let us take up the burden of the day, that we may seek a more abundant reward. Let us not be idle workers, for lo! our Lord has hired us for His vineyard. Let us be planted as vines in the midst of His vineyard, for it is the true vineyard. Let us be fruitful vines, that we may not be uprooted out of His vineyard. Let us be a sweet odour, that our fragrance may breathe forth to all around. Let us be poor in the world, and let us enrich many by the doctrine of our Lord. Let us not call anyone our father in the earth, that we may be the children of the Father which is in heaven. Though we have nothing, yet we possess all things. Though no man know us, yet they that have knowledge of us are many. Let us rejoice in our hope at every time, that He Who is our hope and our Redeemer may rejoice in us. Let us judge ourselves righteously and condemn ourselves, that we may not hang down our faces before the judges who shall sit upon thrones and judge the tribes. Let us take to ourselves, as armour for the contest, the preparation of the Gospel. Let us knock at the door of heaven, that it may be opened before us, and we may enter in through it.

Let us diligently ask for mercy, that we may receive whatsoever is necessary for us. Let us seek His Kingdom and His righteousness, that we may receive increase in the land. Let us think upon the things which are above, on the heavenly things, and meditate on them, where Christ has been lifted up and exalted. But let us forsake the world which is not ours, that we may arrive at the place to which we have been invited. Let us raise up our eyes on high, that we may see the splendour which shall be revealed. Let us lift up our wings as eagles, that we may see the body there where it is. Let us prepare as offerings for the King desirable fruits, fasting and prayer. Let us guard His pledge in purity, that He may trust us over all His treasury. For whosoever deals falsely with His pledge, they suffer him not to enter into the treasure-house. Let us be careful of the body of Christ, that our bodies may rise at the sound of the trumpet. Let us hearken to the voice of the bridegroom, that we may go in with Him into the bride-chamber. Let us prepare the marriage-gift for His bridal day, and let us go forth to meet Him with joy. Let us put on holy raiment, that we may recline in the chief place of the elect. Whosoever puts not on wedding raiment, they cast him out into outer darkness. Whosoever excuses himself from the wedding shall not taste the feast. Whosoever loves fields and merchandise, shall be shut out of the city of Saints. Whosoever does not bear fruit in the vineyard, shall be uprooted and cast out to torment. Whosoever has received money from his Lord, let him return it to its Giver with its increase. Whosoever desires to become a merchant, let, him buy for himself the field and the treasure that is in it. Whosoever receives the good seed, let him purge his land from thorns. Whosoever desires to be a fisherman, let him cast forth his net at every time. Whosoever is training for the conflict, let him keep himself from the world. Whosoever wishes to gain the crown, let him run as a winner in the race. Whosoever wishes to go down into the course to contend, let him learn to (contend) against his adversary. Whosoever wishes to go down to the battle, let him take unto him armour wherewith to fight, and let him purify himself at every time. Whosoever adopts the likeness of angels, let him be a stranger to men. Whosoever takes upon him the yoke of the saints, let him remove from him getting and spending. Whosoever desires to gain himself, let him remove from him the gain of the world. Whosoever loves the abode that is in heaven, let him not toil at the building of clay that will fall. Whosoever is expectant of being caught up in the clouds, let him not make for himself adorned chariots. Whosoever is expectant of the marriage-feast of the Bridegroom, let him not love the feast of this present time. Whosoever wishes to have pleasure in the banquet reserved there, let him remove drunkenness from himself. Whosoever prepares himself for the supper, let him not excuse himself, nor be a merchant. Whosoever he be on whom the good seed falls, let him not allow the Evil One to sow tares in him. Whosoever has begun to build a tower, let him count up all the cost thereof. Whosoever builds ought to finish, that he be not a laughing-stock to them that pass by the way. Whosoever sets his building on the rock, let him make its foundations deep, that it may not be cast down by the billows. Whosoever wishes to fly from the darkness, let him walk while he has light. Whosoever fears to fly in winter, let him prepare himself from the summer-time. Whosoever looks forward to enter into rest, let him make ready his provision for the Sabbath. Whosoever begs forgiveness of his Lord, let him also forgive his debtor. Whosoever does not demand back a hundred dinars, his Lord forgives him ten thousand talents. Whosoever casts down his Lord's money on the banker's table, will not be called an unprofitable servant. Whosoever loves humility, shall be heir in the land of life. Whosoever wishes to make peace, shall be one of the sons of God. Whosoever knows the will of his Lord, let him do that will, that he may not be beaten much. Whosoever cleanses his heart from deceits, His eyes shall behold the King in his beauty. Whosoever receives the Spirit of Christ, let him adorn his inner man. Whosoever is called the temple of God, let him purify his body from all uncleanness. Whosoever grieves the Spirit of Christ, shall not raise up his head from griefs. Whosoever receives the body of Christ, let him keep his body from all uncleanness. Whosoever casts off the old man, let him not turn back to his former works. Whosoever puts on the new man, let him keep himself from all filthiness. Whosoever has put on armour from the water (of baptism), let him not put off his armour that he may not be condemned. Whosoever takes up the shield against the Evil One, let him keep himself from the darts which he hurls at him. Whosoever shall draw back, his Lord has no pleasure in him. Whosoever thinks upon the Law of his Lord, shall not be troubled with the thoughts of this world. Whosoever meditates on the Law of his Lord, is like a tree planted by the waters. Whosoever again has trust in his Lord, is like a tree that is set out by the river. Whosoever puts his trust in man shall receive the curses of Jeremiah. Whosoever is invited to the Bridegroom, let him prepare himself. Whosoever has lighted his lamp, let him not suffer it to go out. Whosoever is expectant of the marriage-cry, let him take oil in his vessel. Whosoever is keeper of the door, let him be on the watch for his Master. Whosoever loves virginity, let him become like Elijah. Whosoever takes up the yoke of the Saints, let him sit and be silent. Whosoever loves peace, let him look for his Master as the hope of life.

2. For, my beloved, our adversary is skilful. He that contends against us is crafty. Against the brave and the renowned does he prepare himself, that they may be weakened. For the feeble are his own, nor does he fight with the captivity that are made captive to him. He that has wings flees from him and the darts that he hurls at him do not reach him. They that are spiritual see him when he assails, and his panoply has no power upon their bodies. All the children of light are without fear of him, because the darkness flies from before the light. The children of the Good fear not the Evil, for He hath given him to be trampled by their feet. When he makes himself like darkness unto them, they become light. And when he creeps upon them like a serpent, they become salt, whereof he cannot eat. If he makes himself like the asp unto them, then

they become like babes. If he comes in upon them in the lust of food, they, like our Redeemer, conquer him by fasting. And if he wishes to contend with them by the lust of the eyes, they lift up their eyes to the height of heaven. If he wishes by enticements to overcome them, they do not afford him a hearing. If he wishes openly to strive with them, lo! they are clothed in panoply and stand up against him. If he wishes to come in against them by sleep, they are wakeful and vigilant and sing psalms and pray. If he allures them by possessions, they give them to the poor. If he comes in as sweetness against them, they taste it not, knowing that he is bitter. If he inflames them with the desire of Eve, they dwell alone, and not with the daughters of Eve.

3. For it was through Eve that he came in upon Adam, and Adam was enticed because of his inexperience. And again he came in against Joseph through his master's wife, but Joseph was acquainted with his craftiness and would not afford him a hearing. Through a woman he fought with Samson, until he took away his Nazariteship. Reuben was the first-born of all his brethren, and through his father's wife, (the adversary) cast a blemish upon him. Aaron was the great high-priest of the house of Israel, and through Miriam his sister he envied Moses. Moses was sent to deliver the people from Egypt, and took with him the woman who advised him to shameful acts, and the Lord met with Moses, and desired to slay him, till he sent back his wife to Midian. David was victorious in all his battles, yet through means of a daughter of Eve there was found a blemish in him. Amnon was beautiful and fair in countenance, yet (the adversary) took him captive by desire for his sister, and Absalom slew him on account of the humbling of Tamar. Solomon was greater than all the kings of the earth, yet in the days of his old age his wives led his heart astray. Through Jezebel, daughter of Ethbaal, the wickedness of Ahab was increased, and he became altogether a heathen. Furthermore, the adversary tempted Job through his children and his possessions, and when he could not prevail over him, he went and brought against him his armour, and he came, bringing with him a daughter of Eve, who had caused Adam to sink, and through her mouth he said to Job, her righteous husband:—Curse God. But Job rejected her counsel. King Asa also conquered the Accursed-of-life, when he wished to come in against him, through his mother. For Asa knew his craftiness and removed his mother from her high estate, and cut in pieces her idol and cast it down. John was greater than all the prophets, yet Herod slew him because of the dancing of a daughter of Eve. Haman was wealthy and third in honour from the King, yet his wife counselled him to destroy the Jews. Zimri was head of the tribe of Simeon, yet Cozbi, daughter of the chiefs of Midian, overthrew him, and because of one woman twenty-four thousand of Israel fell in one day.

4. Therefore, my brethren, if any man who is a monk or a saint, who loves the solitary life, yet desires that a woman, bound by monastic vow like himself, should dwell with him, it would be better for him in that case to take (to wife) a woman openly and not be made wanton by lust. So also again the woman, if she be not separated from the solitary, it is better for her to marry openly. Woman then ought to dwell with woman, and man to dwell with man. And also whatever man desires to continue in holiness, let not his spouse dwell with him, lest he turn back to his former condition, and so be esteemed an adulterer. Therefore this counsel is becoming and right and good, that I give to myself and you, my beloved solitaries, who do not take wives, and to the virgins who do not marry, and to those who have loved holiness. It is just and right and becoming, that even if a man should be distressed, he should continue alone. And thus it becomes him to dwell, as it is written in the Prophet Jeremiah:—Blessed is the man who shall take up Thy yoke in his youth, and sit alone and be silent, because he has taken upon him Thy yoke. For thus, my beloved, it becomes him who takes up the yoke of Christ, to preserve his yoke in purity.

5. For thus it is written, my beloved, concerning Moses, that from the time the Holy One was revealed to him, he also loved holiness. And from the time he was sanctified, his wife ministered not to him. But it is thus written:—Joshua, the son of Nun, was the minister of Moses from his childhood. And of Joshua again it is thus written concerning him, that he used not to depart from the tabernacle. And the temporal tabernacle was not ministered to by a woman, because the Law did not allow women to enter the temporal tabernacle, but even when they came to pray, they used to pray at the door of the temporal tabernacle, and then turn back. Moreover, he commanded the Priests, that at the time of their ministry they should continue in holiness, and should not know their wives. And also concerning Elijah it is thus written, that at one time he dwelt in Mount Carmel, and at another he dwelt at the brook Cherith, and was ministered to by his disciple; and because his heart was in heaven, the bird of heaven used to bring sustenance to him; and because he took upon him the likeness of the angels of heaven, those very angels brought him bread and water when he was fleeing from before Jezebel. And because he set all his thought in heaven, he was caught up in the chariot of fire to heaven, and there his dwelling-place was established for ever. Elisha also walked in the footsteps of his Master. He used to dwell in the upper chamber of the Shunamite, and was ministered to by his disciple. For thus the Shunamite said;—He is a holy Prophet of God and passes by us continually, for thus it becomes his holiness that we should make for him an upper chamber and do for him the service that is (necessary) in it. Now what was the service necessary in the upper chamber

of Elisha? Clearly the bed and table and stool and lamp-stand only. But what shall we say of John? He also used to dwell amongst men, and preserved his virginity honourably, and received the Spirit of God. Moreover, the blessed Apostle said concerning himself and concerning Barnabas:—Had we then not power to eat and to drink and to lead about wives with us? But it was not becoming or right.

6. Therefore, brethren, because we know and have seen that from the beginning it was through woman that the adversary had access unto men, and to the end he will accomplish it by her—for she is the weapon of Satan, and through her he fights against the champions. Through her he makes music at every time, for she became as a harp for him from the first day. For because of her the curse of the Law was established, and because of her the promise unto death was made. For with pangs she bears children and delivers them to death. Because of her the earth was cursed, that it should bring forth thorns and tares. Accordingly, by the coming of the offspring of the Blessed Mary the thorns are uprooted, the sweat wiped away, the fig-tree cursed, the dust made salt, the curse nailed to the cross, the edge of the sword removed from before the tree of life and it given as food to the faithful, and Paradise promised to the blessed and to virgins and to the saints. So the fruit of the tree of life is given as food to the faithful and to virgins, and to those that do the will of God has the door been opened and the way made plain. And the fountain flows and gives drink to the thirsty. The table is laid and the supper prepared. The fatted ox is slain and the cup of redemption mixed. The feast is prepared and the Bridegroom at hand, soon to take his place. The apostles have given the invitation and the called are very many. O ye chosen, prepare yourselves. The light has shone forth both bright and fair, and garments not made with hands are prepared. The marriage cry is at hand. The tombs will be opened and the treasures laid bare. The dead shall rise and the living shall fly to meet the King. The banquet is laid, and the cornet shall encourage and the trumpets shall hasten (them). The Watchers of heaven shall speed, and the throne shall be set for the Judge. He that laboured shall rejoice, and he that was unprofitable shall fear. He that did evil shall not draw nigh unto the Judge. Those on the right hand shall exult, and those on the left shall weep and wail. Those that are in the light shall be glorified, and those that are in the darkness shall groan that they may moisten their tongue. Grace has gone by, and justice reigns. There is no repentance in that place. Winter is at hand; the summer has passed away. The Sabbath of rest has come; toil has ceased. Night has passed away; the light reigns. As to death, its sting is broken and it is swallowed up in life. Those that return to Sheol shall weep and gnash their teeth, and those that go to the

Kingdom shall rejoice and exult and dance and sing praises. For those that take not wives shall be ministered to by the Watchers of heaven. Those that preserve chastity shall rest in the sanctuary of the Most High. The Only Begotten Who is from the bosom of His Father shall cause all the solitaries to rejoice. There is there neither male nor female, neither bond nor free, but they all are the children of the Most High. And all the pure virgins who are betrothed to Christ shall light their lamps and with the Bridegroom shall they go into the marriage chamber. All those that are betrothed to Christ are far removed from the curse of the Law, and are redeemed from the condemnation of the daughters of Eve; for they are not wedded to men so as to receive the curses and come into the pains. They take no thought of death, because they do not deliver children to him. And in place of a mortal husband, they are betrothed to Christ. And because they do not bear children, there is Given to them the name that is better than sons and daughters. And instead of the groans of the daughters of Eve, they utter the songs of the Bridegroom. The wedding-feast of the daughters of Eve continues for but seven days; but for these (virgins) is the Bridegroom who departs not for ever. The adornment of the daughters of Eve is wool that wears out and perishes, but the garments of these wear not out. Old age withers the beauty of the daughters of Eve, but the beauty of these shall be renewed in the time of the Resurrection.

7. O ye virgins who have betrothed yourselves to Christ, when one of the monks shall say to one of you, "I will live with thee and minister thou to me," thus shalt thou say unto him:—"To a royal husband am I betrothed, and Him do I serve; and if I leave His service and serve thee, my betrothed will be wroth with me, and will write me a letter of divorce, and will send me away from His house; and while thou seekest to be honoured by me, and I to be honoured by thee, take heed lest hurt come upon me and thee. Take not fire into thy bosom, lest it burn thy garments; but be thou in honour alone, and I also alone will abide in my honour. And as concerning these things which the Bridegroom has prepared for the eternity of his marriage feast, do thou make thee a wedding-gift and prepare thyself to meet Him. And as for me, I will make me ready oil, that I may enter in with the wise virgins and may not be kept outside the door with the foolish virgins."

8. Hearken then, my beloved, unto that which I write unto thee, namely, whatsoever things become solitaries, monks, virgins, saints. Before all things it beseems the man on whom the yoke is laid, that his faith should be firm; as I wrote to thee in the first epistle; that he should be zealous in fasting and prayer; that he should be fervent in the love of Christ; and should be humble and mild and wise. And let his speech be peaceful and pleasant, and his thought be

sincere with all. Let him speak his words duly weighing them, and set a barrier to his mouth from harmful words, and let him put far from him hasty laughter. Let him not love the adornment of garments, nor again does it become him to let his hair grow long and adorn it, or to anoint it with sweet-scented unguents. Let him not recline at feastings, nor does it become him to wear gorgeous apparel. Let him not dare to exceed at wine. Let him put far from him proud thoughts. It does not become him to look upon gorgeous apparel, or to wear fine raiment. Let him put away from him a crafty tongue; let him drive from him envy and wrath, and cast away from him crafty lips. The words that are spoken about a man, when he about whom they are spoken is not near, let him not hear nor receive, that he sin not, until he search them out. Mockery is a hateful fault, and to bring it up upon the heart is not right. Let him not lend and take interest, and let him not love avarice. Let him suffer wrong and not do wrong. Furthermore, let him put away from him turmoil, and words of jesting let him not utter. Let him not scorn any man who is repenting of his sins, and let him not mock his brother who is fasting, and him that cannot fast let him not put to shame. Where he is received, let him reprove, and where they receive him not, let him understand his own honour. In an acceptable time let him speak his word; otherwise, let him be silent. Let him not for his belly's sake make himself despised by his begging, and to such an one as fears God let him reveal his secret; but let him keep himself from the evil (man). Let him not speak in complaisance with a wicked man, nor with his enemy. And so let him contend as to have no enemy at all. When men envy him in that which is good, let him add to his goodness, and let him not be harmed because of envy. When he has, and gives to the poor, let him rejoice; and when he has not, let it not grieve him. With a wicked man let him have no converse and with a contemptuous man let him not speak, lest he give himself to contempt. With a blasphemer let him not dispute, lest his Lord be blasphemed on his account. Let him depart from a slanderer, and let no man please another man with speciousness of words. These things beseem solitaries who take up the heavenly yoke, and become disciples of Christ. For thus it befits the disciples of Christ to be like unto Christ their Master.

9. Let us take pattern, my beloved, from our Saviour, Who though He was rich, made Himself poor; and though He was lofty, humbled His Majesty; and though His dwelling place was in heaven, He had no place to lay His head; and though He is to come upon the clouds, yet rode on a colt and so entered Jerusalem; and though He is God and Son of God, He took upon Him the likeness of a servant; and though He was (for others) rest from all weariness, yet was Himself tired with the weariness of the journey; though He was the

fountain that quenches thirst, yet Himself thirsted and asked for water; though He was abundance and satisfied our hunger, yet He Himself hungered when He went forth to the wilderness to be tempted; though He was a Watcher that slumbers not, He yet slumbered and slept in the ship in the midst of the sea; and though He was ministered to in the Tabernacle of His Father, yet let Himself be served by the hands of men; though He was the healer of all sick men, yet nails were fastened into His hands; though His mouth brought forth things that were good, yet they gave Him gall to eat; though He injured no man and harmed none, yet He was beaten with stripes and endured shame; and though he was Saviour of all mortals, He delivered Himself to the death of the cross.

10. All this humility did our Saviour show us in Himself. Let us then also humble ourselves, my beloved. When our Lord went outside of His nature, He walked in our nature. Let us abide in our nature, that in the day of judgment He may cause us to partake of His nature. Our Lord took from us a pledge when He went, and He left us a pledge of His own when he ascended. He that was without need, because of our need devised this expedient. What was ours was His even from the beginning, but that which was His, who would have given us? But true is that which our Lord promised us:—Where I am there ye also shall be. For whatsoever He took of ours, is in honour with Him, and (as) a diadem is bound upon His Head. So also that, which of His we have received, we ought to honour. That which is ours is held in honour with Him who was not in our nature: let us honour that which is His in His own nature. If we honour Him, we shall go to Him, Who took upon Him of our nature and so ascended. But if we despise Him, He will take away from us that which He has given us. If we deal fraudulently with His pledge, He will there take away that which is His, and will deprive us of all that He has promised us. Let us magnify gloriously the King's Son Who is with us, because a hostage for Him has been taken from us. Whoso holds the King's Son in honour, shall obtain many gifts from the King. That of ours, that is with Him, has sat down in honour and a diadem is bound upon His head, and He has sat down with the King. And we who are poor, what shall we do to the King's Son Who is with us? He needs nothing from us, but that we should adorn our temples for Him; that when the time is accomplished and He goes to His Father, He may give thanks to Him because of us, because we have honoured Him. When He came to us, He had nothing of ours, and also we had nothing of His, though the two natures were His and His Father's. For when Gabriel made announcement to the Blessed Mary who bore Him, the word from on high set out and came, and the word became flesh and dwelt in us. And when He

returned to Him that sent Him, He took away, when He went, that which He had not brought, as the Apostle said:—He has taken us up and seated us with Himself in the heavens. And when He went to His Father, He sent to us His Spirit and said to us I am with you till the world shall end. For Christ sitteth at the right hand of His Father, and Christ dwelleth among men. He is sufficient above and beneath, by the wisdom of His Father. And He dwells in many, though He is one, and all the faithful each by each He overshadows from Himself, and fails not, as it is written:—I will divide Him among many. And though He is divided among many, yet He sits at the right hand of His Father. And He is in us and we are in Him, as He said:—Ye are in Me and I am in you. And in another place He said:—I and Father are one.

11. And if anyone, whose conscience lacks knowledge, should dispute about this and say:—"Since Christ is one and His Father is one, how does Christ dwell, and His Father dwell, in faithful men? And how do righteous men become temples for God that He should dwell in them? If then it is thus, that to each several faithful man there comes a several Christ, and God Who is in Christ,—if it is so, there are for them Gods many and Christs without number." But hear, my beloved, the defence that is suited to this argument. From that which is visible let him that has thus said receive instruction. For every man knows that the sun is fixed in the heavens, yet its rays are spread out in the earth, and (light) from it enters by many doors and windows of houses; and wherever the sunshine falls, though it be but as (the measure of) the palm of the hand, it is called the sun. And though it fall in many places, it is thus called, but the real sun itself is in heaven. Therefore, if it is so, have they many suns? Also the water of the sea is vast, and when thou takest one cup from it, that is called water. And though thou shouldest divide it into a thousand vessels, yet it is called water by its name. Also when thou kindlest fire from fire in many places, the place from whence thou takest it, when thou kindlest it, lacks not, and the fire is called by one name. And because thou dividest it into many places, it does not on that account become possessed of many names. And when thou takest dust from the earth, and castest it into many places, it is not a whit diminished, and also thou canst not call it by many names. Thus also God and His Christ, though they are One, yet dwell in men who are many. And they are in heaven in person, and are diminished in nothing when they dwell in many; as the sun is not a whit diminished in heaven, when its power is poured out in the earth. How much greater then is the power of God, since by the power of God the very sun itself subsists.

12. Again I will remind thee, my beloved, also of that which is written. For thus it is written, that when it was a grievous burden to Moses to lead the

camp alone, the Lord said to him:—Lo! will take away of the Spirit that is upon thee, and will put it upon seventy men, elders of Israel. But when He took away some of the Spirit of Moses, and the seventy men were filled with it, Moses nothing lacked, nor could it be known that anything was taken away from his Spirit. Moreover the blessed apostle also said:—God divided of the Spirit of Christ and sent it into the Prophets. And Christ was in nothing injured, for it was not by measure that His Father gave unto Him the Spirit. By this reflection thou canst comprehend that Christ dwells in faithful men; yet Christ suffers no loss though He is divided among many. For the Prophets received of the Spirit of Christ, each one of them as he was able to bear. And of the Spirit of Christ again there is poured forth to-day upon all flesh, and the sons and the daughters prophesy, the old men and the youths, the men-servants and the hand-maids. Something of Christ is in us, yet Christ is in heaven at the right hand of His Father. And Christ received the Spirit not by measure, but His Father loved Him and delivered all into His hands, and gave Him authority over all His treasure. For John said:—Not by measure did the Father give the Spirit to His Son, but loved Him and gave all into His hands. And also our Lord said:—All things have been delivered unto Me by My Father. Again he said:—The Father will not judge any man, but all judgment will He give unto His Son. Again also the Apostle said:—Everything shall be made subject unto Christ except His Father Who hath subjected all unto Him. And when everything is made subject unto Him by the Father, then He also shall be made subject to God His Father Who subjected all to Him, and God shall be all in all, and in every man.

13. Our Lord testifies concerning John, that he is the greatest of the Prophets. Yet he received the Spirit by limit, because in that measure in which Elijah received the Spirit, (in the same) John obtained it. And as Elijah used to dwell in the wilderness, so also the Spirit of God led John into the wilderness, and he used to dwell in the mountains and caves. The birds sustained Elijah, and John used to eat locusts that fly. Elijah had his loins girded with a girdle of leather; so John had his loins girded with a cincture of leather. Jezebel persecuted Elijah, and Herodias persecuted John. Elijah reproved Ahab, and John reproved Herod. Elijah divided the Jordan, and John opened up baptism. The spirit of Elijah rested twofold upon Elisha, so John laid his hand on our Redeemer, and He received the Spirit not by measure. Elijah opened the heavens and ascended; and John saw the heavens opened, and the Spirit of God which descended and rested upon our Redeemer. Elisha received twofold the Spirit of Elijah; and our Redeemer received that of John and that of heaven. Elisha took the mantle of Elijah, and our Redeemer the imposition of the hand of the

priests. Elisha made oil from water, and our Redeemer made wine from water. Elisha satisfied with a little bread a hundred men only; and our Redeemer satisfied with a little bread five thousand men besides children and women. Elisha cleansed Naaman the leper, and our Redeemer cleansed the ten (lepers). Elisha cursed the children and they were devoured by bears, but our Redeemer blessed the children. The children reviled Elisha, but the children glorified our Redeemer with Hosannas. Elisha cursed Gehazi his servant, and our Redeemer cursed Judas His disciple and blessed all His (other) disciples. Elisha raised to life one dead man only, but our Redeemer raised up three to life. On the bones of Elisha one dead man revived, but when our Saviour descended to the abode of the dead, He quickened many and raised them up. And many are the signs that the Spirit of Christ wrought, which the Prophets received from Him.

14. Therefore, my beloved, we also have received of the Spirit of Christ, and Christ dwelleth in us, as it is written that the Spirit said this through the mouth of the Prophet:—I will dwell in them and will walk in them. Therefore let us prepare our temples for the Spirit of Christ, and let us not grieve it that it may not depart from us. Remember the warning that the Apostle gives us:—Grieve not the Holy Spirit whereby ye have been sealed unto the day of redemption. For from baptism do we receive the Spirit of Christ. For in that hour in which the priests invoke the Spirit, the heavens open and it descends and moves upon the waters. And those that are baptized are clothed in it; for the Spirit stays aloof from all that are born of the flesh, until they come to the new birth by water, and then they receive the Holy Spirit. For in the first birth they are born with an animal souls which is created within man and is not thereafter subject to death, as he said:—Adam became a living soul. But in the second birth, that through baptism, they received the Holy Spirit from a particle of the Godhead, and it is not again subject to death. For when men die, the animal spirit is buried with the body, and sense is taken away from it, but the heavenly spirit that they receive goes according to its nature to Christ. And both these the Apostle has made known, for he said:—The body is buried in animal wise, and rises again in spiritual wise. The Spirit goes back again to Christ according to its nature, for the Apostle said again:—When we shall depart from the body we shall be with our Lord. For the Spirit of Christ, which the spiritual receive, goes to our Lord. And the animal spirit is buried in its nature, and sense is taken away from it. Whosoever guards the Spirit of Christ in purity, when it returns to Christ it thus addresses him:—"The body into which I went, and which put me on from the water of the baptism, has kept me in holiness." And the Holy Spirit will be earnest with Christ for the resurrection of that body which kept Him with purity, and the Spirit will

request to be again conjoined to it that that body may rise up in glory. And whatever man there is that receives the Spirit from the water (of baptism) and grieves it, it departs from him until he dies, and returns according to its nature to Christ, and accuses that man of having grieved it. And when the time of the final consummation shall have come, and the time of the Resurrection shall have approached, the Holy Spirit, that was kept in purity, receives great power from its nature and comes before Christ and stands at the door of the tombs, where the men are buried that kept it in purity, and awaits the (resurrection) shout. And when the Watchers shall have opened the doors of heaven before the King, then the cornet shall summon, and the trumpets shall sound, and the Spirit that waits for the (resurrection) shout shall hear, and quickly shall open the tombs, and raise up the bodies and whatsoever was buried in them, and shall put on the glory that comes with it. And (the Spirit) shall be within for the resurrection of the body, and the glory shall be without for the adornment of the body. And the animal spirit shall be swallowed up in the heavenly Spirit, and the whole man shall become spiritual, since his body is possessed by it (the Spirit). And death shall be swallowed up in life, and body shall be swallowed up in Spirit. And by the power of the Spirit, that man shall fly up to meet the King and He shall receive him with joy, and Christ shall give thanks for the body that has kept His Spirit in purity.

15. This is the Spirit, my beloved, that the Prophets received, and thus also have we received. And it is not at every time found with those that receive it, but sometimes it returns to Him that sent it, and sometimes it goes to him that receives it. Hearken to that which our Lord said:—Despise not one of these little ones that believe on Me, for their angels in heaven do always behold the face of My Father. This Spirit then goes frequently and stands before God and beholds His face, and whosoever injures the temple in which it dwells, it will accuse him before God.

16. I will instruct thee of that which is written, that the Spirit is not at every time found with those that receive it. For thus it is written about Saul, that the Holy Spirit, which he received when he was anointed, departed from him, because he grieved it, and God sent to him instead of it a vexing spirit. And whenever he was afflicted by the evil spirit, David used to play upon the harp, and the Holy Spirit, which David received when he was anointed, would come, and the evil spirit that was vexing Saul, would flee from before it. So the Holy Spirit that David received was not found with him at every time. As long as he was playing the harp, then it used to come. For had it been with him always, it would not have allowed him to sin with the wife of Uriah. For when he was praying about his sins, and was confessing his offences before God, he

said thus:—Take not Thy holy spirit from me. Also concerning Elisha it is thus written, that, while he played upon his harp, then the spirit came to him and he prophesied and said:—Thus saith the Lord, ye shall not see wind nor rain, yet this valley shall be made many pits. And also when the Shunamite came to him because of her son that was dead, he said thus to her:—The Lord hid it from me and did cause me not to know it. Yet, when the King of Israel sent against him to slay him, the Spirit informed him before the messenger came upon him, and he said:—Lo! this son of iniquity has sent to take away my head. And again he made known about the abundance that came about in Samaria the day after. And again the Spirit informed him when Gehazi stole the silver and concealed it.

17. Therefore, my beloved, when the Holy Spirit departs from a man who has received it, until it returns and comes to him, then Satan draws near unto that man, to cause him to sin, and that the Holy Spirit may leave him altogether. For as long as the Spirit is with a man, Satan fears to come near him. And observe, my beloved, that our Lord also, Who was born from the Spirit, was not tempted by Satan until in baptism He received the Spirit from on high. And then the Spirit led him forth to be tempted by Satan. This, then, is the way with man; that in the hour in which he perceives in himself that he is not fervent in the Spirit, and that his heart is inclining to the thought of this world, he may know that the Spirit is not with him, and may arise and pray and keep vigil that the Spirit of God may come to him, that he be not overcome by the adversary. A thief does not dig into a house, until he sees that its master is departing from it. Thus also Satan cannot draw near to that house which is our body, until the Spirit of Christ departs from it. And be sure, my beloved, that the thief does not certainly know whether the master of the house is within or not, but first he applies his ear, and looks. If he hears the voice of the master of the house within it saying:—"I have a journey to go," and when he has searched out and seen that the master of the house has set out to perform his business, then the thief comes and digs into the house and steals. But if he hears the voice of the master of the house admonishing and commanding his household to watch and guard his house, and saying to them, "I also am within the house," then the thief will fear and flee, that he may not be taken and captured. Thus also Satan, he has not the knowledge beforehand to know or see when the Spirit will depart, that so he may come to rob the man; but he too listens and watches, and so assails. But if he hears a man in whom Christ dwells speaking shameful words, or enraged, or quarrelling, or contending, then Satan knows that Christ is not with him, and he comes and accomplishes his will in him. For Christ dwells in the peaceful and the meek,

and lodges in those that fear His word, as He says through the prophet:—On whom shall I look, and in whom shall I dwell, but in the peaceful and the meek who fear My word? And our Lord said:—Whoever walks in My commandments and keeps My love, We will come to him and make Our abode with him. But if he hears from a man that he is on his guard and is praying and meditating in the Law of his Lord by day and by night, then he turns back from him, for he knows that Christ is with him. And if thou shouldest say, "How manifold is Satan! for lo! he fights with many;" then hear and learn from that which I proved to thee above concerning Christ, that no matter to what extent He is divided amongst many, yet He is not a whit diminished. For, as the house, through the window of which a little sunlight enters, is altogether illumined, so the man into whom a little of Satan enters, is altogether darkened. Hear that which the Apostle said:—If Satan is transfigured to an angel of light, it is no wonder if his ministers also are transfigured to ministers of righteousness. And again our Lord said to His disciples:—Lo, I have given you authority to tread upon the power of the adversary. And the Scriptures have made known that he has power and also ministers. Moreover Job said concerning him:—God made him to wage his war. These ministers then that he has, he causes to run in the world, to wage war. But be sure that he will not fight openly; because from the time of the coming of our Saviour, (God) has given authority over him. But he will surely plunder and steal.

18. But I will explain to thee, my beloved, concerning that word which the Apostle said, by which can be weighed the doctrines that are instruments of the Evil One and doctrines of deceit. For the Apostle said:—There is an animal body and there is a spiritual body, seeing that it is thus written:—The first Adam became a living soul and the second Adam a quickening spirit. So they say that there will be two Adams. But he said:—As we have put on the image of that Adam who was from the earth, so we shall put on the image of that Adam who is from heaven. For Adam who was from the earth was he that sinned, and the Adam who is from heaven is our Saviour, our Lord Jesus Christ. They then that receive the Spirit of Christ, come into the likeness of the heavenly Adam, Who is our Saviour, our Lord Jesus Christ. For the animal shall be swallowed up in the spiritual, as I wrote unto thee above. And the man that grieves the spirit of Christ, will be animal in his resurrection; because the heavenly spirit is not with him, that the animal might be swallowed up in it. But when he shall arise he shall continue in his natural state, naked of the Spirit. Because he stripped off from him the Spirit of Christ, he shall be given over to utter nakedness. And whosoever honours the Spirit, and it is guarded in him in purity, in that day the Holy Spirit shall protect him, and he shall

become altogether spiritual, and shall not be found naked; as the Apostle said:—And when we shall have clothed ourselves, may we not be found naked. And again he said:—We shall all sleep, but in the resurrection we shall not all be changed. And again he said:—This which dies shall put on that which dies not, and this which is corruptible that which is incorruptible, and when this which dies shall have put on that which dies not, and this corruptible that which is incorruptible, then shall be accomplished that word which is written that death is swallowed up by victory. Again he said:—Suddenly as the twinkling of an eye, the dead shall rise incorruptible and we shall be changed. And they who shall be changed shall put on the form of that heavenly Adam and shall become spiritual. And those who shall not be changed, shall continue animal in the created nature of Adam, namely, of dust; and shall continue in their nature in the earth below. And then the heavenly shall be caught up to heaven and the Spirit that they have put on shall cause them to fly, and they shall inherit the kingdom that was prepared for them from the beginning. And they that are animal shall remain on the earth by the weight of their bodies, and shall turn back to Sheol, and there shall be weeping and gnashing of teeth.

19. In writing this I have reminded myself, and also thee, my beloved; therefore love virginity, the heavenly portion, the fellowship of the Watchers of heaven. For there is nothing comparable with it. And in those that are thus, in them Christ dwells. The time of summer is at hand, and the fig-tree has budded and its leaves have come out—the signs that our Redeemer gave have begun to be fulfilled. For he said:—People shall rise against people and kingdom against kingdom. And there shall be famines and pestilences and terrors from heaven. And lo! all these things are being accomplished in our days.

20. Therefore read in this whatever I have written unto thee, thou and the brethren, the monks that love virginity. And be on thy guard against scorners. For whosoever scorns and mocks his brother, the word that is written in the Gospel fitly applies to him; namely, when our Lord wished to take account with the avaricious and with the Pharisees. For it is written:—Because they loved money, they mocked Him. So also now those that do not agree with these things mock in the same way. Read then and learn. Be zealous for reading and for doing. And let the Law of God be thy meditation at every time. And when thou hast read this epistle, on thy life (I adjure thee), my beloved, arise and pray, and remember my sinfulness in thy prayer.

Demonstration VIII

Of the Resurrection of the Dead

1. At all times controversies arise on this matter, how the dead shall rise and with what body they shall come? For lo! the body wears out and is corrupted; and the bones also, no doubt, as time lengthens out over them, waste away and are not to be recognised. And when thou enterest a tomb in which a hundred dead men are buried, thou findest not there an handful of dust. And thus say those that reflect on these things:—"We know of course that the dead shall rise; but they will be clothed in a heavenly body and spiritual forms. And if it is not so, these hundred dead that were buried in one tomb, of whom after a long time elapses there remains nothing at all there, when the dead shall be quickened, and shall be clothed in a body and rise, unless they shall be clothed in a heavenly body, from whence shall their body come? For lo! there is nothing in the tomb."

2. Whosoever reflects thus is foolish, and without knowledge. When the dead were brought in, they were something; and when they were there for a long time, they became nothing. And, when the time shall have come that the dead shall rise, that nothing shall become something according to its former nature, and a change shall be added to its nature. O thou unwise who reflectest thus, hear that which the blessed Apostle said when he was instructing a foolish man like thee; for he said:—Thou fool, the seed which thou sowest unless it die is not quickened; and that which thou sowest is not like that which grows up into blade, but one bare grain of wheat or barley or some other seedling. And to each one of the seeds is given its own body. But God clothes thy seed with its body as He wills.

3. Therefore, O fool, be instructed by this, that each of the seeds is clothed in its own body. Never dost thou sow wheat and yet reap barley, and never dost thou plant a vine and yet it produced figs; but everything grows according to its nature. Thus also the body that was laid in the earth is that which shall

rise again. And as to this, that the body is corrupted and wastes away, thou oughtest to be instructed by the parable of the seed; that as the seed, when it is cast into the earth, decays and is corrupted, and from its decay it produces and buds and bears fruit. For the land that is ploughed, into which seed is not cast, produces not fruit, even if that land drinks in all the rain. So the grave in which the dead are not buried, from it men shall not issue forth in the quickening of the dead, though the full voice of the trumpet should sound within it. And if, as they say, the spirit of the just shall ascend into heaven and put on a heavenly body, they are in heaven. And He Who raises the dead dwells in heaven. Then when our Saviour shall come, whom shall He raise up from the earth? And why did He write for us:—The hour shall come, and now is, that the dead also shall hear the voice of the Son of Man, and they shall live and come forth from their tombs? For the heavenly body will not come and enter into the tomb, and again go forth from it.

4. For thus say those who are stubborn in folly:—Why did the Apostle say,—Different is the body which is in heaven from that which is on earth? But he that hears this, let him hear also the other thing that the Apostle said:—There is an animal body, and there is a spiritual body. And again he said:—We shall all sleep, but we shall not all be changed. And again he said:—This that shall die must clothe itself with that that shall not die, and this which is corruptible must clothe itself with that which is incorruptible. Again he said:—We must all stand before the judgment-seat of Christ, that every man may be rewarded in his body for everything that before time was done by him, whether good or evil. Again he said:—What shall those do that are baptized for the dead? For if the dead rise not, why are they baptized for them? Again he said:—If there is no resurrection of the dead, then is Christ not risen, and if Christ is not risen then your faith is vain, and our preaching. And if so we are found false witnesses in that we testified of God, that He raised up Christ, Whom He raised not up. Therefore, if the dead rise not, there is no judgment. And if there is no judgment, then let us eat and drink, for to-morrow we shall die. Be not deceived; evil communications corrupt good purposes. Now as to this that the Apostle said:—The body that is in heaven is different from that which is on the earth, let this word be thus understood by thee. When the body of the just shall arise and be changed, it is called heavenly. And that which is not changed is called earthly, according to its earthly nature.

5. But hear, my beloved, another word like this, which the Apostle has spoken. For he said:—The spiritual man judgeth everything, and he is judged by no one. And again he said:—They that are spiritual are spiritually minded, and they that are carnal are carnally minded. And again he said:—When we were

in the flesh, the weaknesses of sins were working in our members that we might become fruit for death. Again he said:—If the Spirit of Christ is in you, ye are spiritual. All these things the Apostle said, while he was clothed in the flesh but was doing the works of the Spirit. Thus also in the Resurrection of the dead, the righteous shall be changed, and the earthly form shall be swallowed up in the heavenly, and it shall be called a heavenly body. And that which shall not be changed, shall be called earthly.

6. Concerning then this Resurrection of the dead, my beloved, according to my power I will instruct thee. For from the beginning God created Adam; moulded him from the dust of the earth, and raised him up. For if, while Adam was not, He made him from nothing, how much easier now is it for Him to raise him up; for lo! as a seed he is sown in the earth. For if God should do those things that are easy for us, His works would not appear mighty to us. For lo! there are amongst men artificers who make wonderful things, and those who are not artificers of the works stand and wonder how they were done; and the work of their fellows is difficult in their eyes. How much more should not the works of God be as a marvel! But for God this was no great thing, that the dead should be quickened. Before seed was sown in the earth, the earth produced that which had not been cast into it. Before it had conceived, it bore in its virginity. How then is this difficult, that the earth should cause to spring up again what had been cast into it, and after conception should bear? And lo! her travail-pains are near; as Isaiah said, Who hath seen anything like this and who hath heard such things as these? that the earth should travail in one day, and a people should be born in one hour? For Adam unsown sprang up; unconceived he was born. But lo! now his offspring are sown, and wait for the rain, and shall spring up. And lo! the earth teems with many, and the time of her bringing forth is at hand.

7. For all our fathers, in hope of the Resurrection and the quickening of the dead, were looking forward and hastening; as the blessed Apostle said, If the righteous had been looking forward to that city from which Abraham went forth, they would have had an opportunity of again turning back and to it; but they showed that they were looking forward to one better than it, namely that which is in heaven. They were looking forward to be released and to go speedily thither. And from that which I am writing unto thee, understand and observe that they were looking forward to the Resurrection. For Jacob our father, when he was dying, bound Joseph his son with an oath, and said to him, Bury me in the tomb of my fathers, with Abraham and Sarah and Isaac and Rebecca. And why, my beloved, did Jacob not wish to be buried in Egypt, but with his fathers? He showed beforehand, that he was looking forward to

the quickening of the dead; that, when the Resurrection shout should be raised and the sound of the trumpet (heard), he might rise up near to his fathers, and might not at the time of the Resurrection be mingled with the wicked who shall return to Sheol and to punishment.

8. Thus also Joseph bound his brethren by an oath, and said to them:—When God shall remember you, take up my bones from hence with you. And according to the word of Joseph his brethren did, and kept the oath a hundred and twenty-five years. At that time when the hosts of the Lord went out from the land of Egypt, then Moses took up the bones of Joseph when he went forth. And the bones of the righteous man were more precious and better in his estimation than the gold and the silver that the children of Israel took from Egypt when they spoiled them. And the bones of Joseph were forty years in the wilderness; and at that time when Moses fell asleep, he gave them in inheritance to Joshua the son of Nun. The bones of Joseph his father were better in his estimation than all the spoil of that land which he subdued. And why did Moses give the bones of Joseph to Joshua? Clearly, because he was of the tribe of Ephraim the son of Joseph. And he buried them in the land of promise, that there might be in that land a treasure, (even) that of the bones of Joseph (that were) buried therein. And also at the time that Jacob was dying, he blessed his tribes, and showed them what would happen to them in the latter days, and said to Reuben:—Reuben, thou art my firstborn, might and the beginning of my strength. Thou hast gone astray; as water, thou shalt not abide, because thou wentest up father's bed. Truly thou defilest my couch and wentest up. From the time that Jacob fell asleep until the time that Moses fell asleep two hundred and thirty-three years elapsed. Then Moses wished by his priestly power to absolve Reuben from his transgression and sin, in that he had lain with Bilhah, his father's concubine; that when his brethren should rise, he might not be cut off from their number. So he said in the beginning of his blessing:—Reuben shall live and not die, and shall be in the number.

9. And also when the time came that Moses should sleep with his fathers, he was grieved and distressed, and he sought of his Lord and entreated that he might pass over to the land of promise. And why, my beloved, was the righteous Moses grieved because he did not enter into the land of promise? Clearly, because he wished to go and be buried with his fathers, and not be buried in the land of his adversaries, in the land of Moab. For the Moabites hired Balaam the son of Beor to curse Israel. Therefore Moses wished not to be buried in that land, lest the Moabites should come and take vengeance on him by taking up and casting forth the bones of that righteous man. And the Lord performed an act of grace towards Moses. For He brought him forth to Mount

Nebo, and showed him all the land, making it pass before him. And as Moses gazed upon all the land, and gazed upon the mountain of the Jebusites where the Tabernacle was to dwell, he was grieved and wept when he saw the tomb in Hebron where his fathers Abraham, Isaac and Jacob were buried, that he should not be buried with them, nor his bones cast upon their bones, that he might rise along with them in the Resurrection. But when he had seen all the land, his Lord encouraged him and said to him, "I myself will bury thee and hide thee, and none shall know thy tomb." So Moses died according to the word of the mouth of the Lord, and He buried him in a valley in the land of Moab over against Beth-Peor, where Israel had sinned, and no man has known his sepulchre unto this day. Two goodly benefits did his Lord accomplish for Moses in not making known his tomb to the children of Israel. He rejoiced that his adversaries should not know it, and cast forth his bones from his tomb; and in the second place, that the children of his people should not know it, and make his tomb a place of worship, for he was accounted as God in the eyes of the children of his people. And understand this, my beloved, from hence, that when he left them and went up to the mountain, they said:—As for this Moses who brought us up from the land of Egypt we know not what has become of him. So they made them a calf and worshipped it, and they remembered not God Who brought them up from Egypt by means of Moses with a mighty hand and an uplifted arm. Because of this, God had respect unto Moses, and did not make known his tomb; lest, if He should make known his tomb, the children of his people might go astray, and make them an image, and worship it and sacrifice to it, and so by their sins disquiet the bones of the righteous man.

10. And Moses again proclaimed clearly the Resurrection of the dead, for he said as from the mouth of his God:—It is I that cause to die and it is I that make alive. Again also Hannah said thus in her prayer:—The Lord causeth to die and quickeneth; He bringeth down to Sheol and bringeth up (therefrom). The Prophet Isaiah also said thus:—Thy dead shall live, O Lord, and their bodies shall rise, and they that sleep in the dust shall awake and praise thee. David also proclaimed, saying:—For lo! for the dead Thou workest wonderful things, and the mighty ones shall rise and make confession unto Thee, and those that are in the tombs shall recount Thy grace. And how in the tombs shall they recount the grace of God? Clearly, when they shall hear the sound of trumpet summoning them, and the cornet sounding forth from on high, and the earthquake that shall be, and the tombs that shall be opened, then the mighty ones shall arise in glory, and recount one to another in the tombs, saying, "Great is the grace that is performed towards us. For our hope was cut

off; yet (another) hope has arisen for us. We were imprisoned in darkness, and have come forth to the light. We were sown in corruption, and have risen in glory. We were buried naturally, and we have risen spiritually. Again we were sown in weakness, and have risen in power." This is the grace that they shall tell of in the tombs.

11. And it was not only in words, my beloved, that God said:—"I quicken the dead," but also in deeds He showed it to us by many testimonies; that we might have no hesitation (concerning it). He showed it beforehand plainly; for through Elijah a wonder was manifested, (in proof) that the dead shall live and that they that sleep in the dust shall arise. For when the son of the widow died, Elijah raised him up and gave him to his mother. And Elisha again, his disciple, raised up the son of the Shunamite; that the testimony of two might be established and confirmed for us. And also again when the children of Israel cast a dead man on the bones of Elisha, that dead man revived and arose. And the witness of three is certain.

12. And also through the Prophet Ezekiel, the Resurrection of the dead was manifestly shown, when God brought him forth to the valley and showed him many bones, and made him pass by them round about them, and said to him:—Son of Man, will these bones live? And Ezekiel said to Him:—Thou knowest, O Lord of lords. And the Lord said to him:—Prophesy, O Son Man, over these bones; prophesy and say to the dry bones, Hear the word of the Lord of lords. And when he had caused them to hear those words, there was a shaking and a noise, and the bones were gathered together, even those that were crushed into pieces and broken. And when the Prophet saw them, he was astonished, for they came together from all sides, and each bone received its fellow, and each joint approached its fellow-joint, and they ordered themselves, one on another. And their dryness was made moist, and the joints were united by the ligatures, and the blood grew warm in the arteries, and skin was stretched over the flesh, and hair grew up according to its nature. But they lay prostrate and there was no breath in them. Then again He commanded the Prophet, and said to him:—Prophesy unto the spirit and say to it, Come, O spirit, from the four winds, and breathe upon these slain men that they may live. And when he caused them to hear this second word, the spirit entered into them, and they revived and stood up upon their feet, a very great host.

13. But why, my beloved, was it that those dead did not rise because of the one word (spoken) through Ezekiel, and why was not their resurrection, both of bones and spirit, accomplished (through that one word)? For lo! by one word the bones were fitted together, and by another the spirit came. It was in order that full perfection might be left for our Lord Jesus Christ, Who with

one utterance and one word will raise up at the last day every body of man. For it was not the word that was insufficient, but its bearer was inferior. And with regard to this, understand and observe that when Elijah also, and Elisha his disciple, raised the dead, it was not with one word that they raised them up, but after they had prayed and made intercession and delayed no little time, then they arose.

14. And our Lord Himself, in that His first Coming raised up three that were dead, that the testimony of three might be made sure. And He raised up each one of them with two words each. For when He raised up the widow's son, He called him twice, saying to him, Young man, young man, arise. And he revived and arose. And again, He twice called the daughter of the chief of the synagogue, saying to her, Damsel, damsel, arise. And her spirit returned and she arose. And after Lazarus died, when He came to the place of burial. He prayed earnestly and cried with a loud voice and said, Lazarus, come forth. And he revived and came out of his tomb.

15. And concerning all this that I have explained to thee, that those dead persons were raised with two words each, it was because for them two resurrections take place; that former one, and the second, that which is to come. For in that resurrection in which all men shall rise, none shall fall again; and by one word of God, sent forth through Christ, all the dead shall rise in the twinkling of an eye, speedily. For He Who brings it to pass is not feeble or insufficient. For with one word of summons He will cause all the ends (of the world) to hear, and all that are laid (in the grave) shall leap forth and rise up; and no word shall return void to Him that sent it forth, but as it is written in the Prophet Isaiah, who compares the word to rain and snow; for he said:—As the rain and the snow come down from heaven and return not thither, but fertilize the earth and cause it to bring forth and give seed to the sower and bread for food, so shall the word be that goes forth from My mouth, and it shall not return to Me void, but shall accomplish whatsoever I desire and shall accomplish that for which I shall have sent it. For the rain and the snow do not return to heaven, but accomplish in the earth the will of Him that sends them. So the word that He shall send through His Christ, Who is Himself the Word and the Message, shall return to Him with great power. For when He shall come and bring it, He shall come down like rain and snow, and through Him all that is sown shall spring up and bear righteous fruit, and the word shall return to His sender; but not in vain shall His going have been, but thus shall He say in the presence of His sender:—Behold, I and the children that the Lord has given Me. And this is the voice through which the dead shall live. Concerning it our Redeemer testifies, saying:—The hour shall come when

even the dead shall hear the voice of the Son of Man and shall come forth from their tombs; as it is written, In the beginning was the voice, that is the Word. Again He said, The Word became a body and dwelt amongst us. And this is that voice of God which shall sound from on high and raise up all the dead.

16. Again, our Lord explained to the Sadducees with regard to the resurrection of the dead, when they brought forth to Him the parable of the woman who was married to seven husbands, and said to Him:—Lo! the woman was wife of them all; in the Resurrection of the dead, to which of them shall she be wife? Then our Lord said to them:—Ye do greatly err, and ye know not the Scriptures nor the power of God. For they who are worthy of that world and of that Resurrection from the dead, they that are men do not take wives, nor are the women married to husbands, for they cannot die, for they are as the angels of God and children of the Resurrection. But concerning the Resurrection, that the dead shall rise, have ye not read in the Scripture that God said to Moses out of the bush, "I am the God of Abraham, of Isaac and of Jacob." And lo! He is not God of the dead, for they all are alive unto Him.

17. And there are those who even while they live are dead unto God. For He laid a commandment on Adam and said to him, In the day that thou shalt eat of the tree, thou shalt surely die. And after he had transgressed the commandment, and had eaten, he lived nine hundred and thirty years; but he was accounted dead unto God because of his sins. But that it may be made certain for thee that a sinner is called dead even when he lives, I will make it clear to thee. For thus it is written in Ezekiel the Prophet, As I live, saith the Lord of lords, I desire not the death of the dead sinner.

18. Moreover our Lord said to that man who said to Him:—Let me go and bury my father, and I will come to Thee. And our Lord said to him, Let the dead bury their dead, but go thou, preach the Kingdom of God. But how is this word understood by thee, my beloved? Didst thou ever see the dead burying their dead? Or how shall a dead man arise to bury another dead man? But receive this explanation from me, that a sinner, while he is living, is dead unto God; and a righteous man, though dead, is alive unto God. For such death is a sleep, as David said, I lay down and slept, and awoke. Again Isaiah said, They that sleep in the dust shall awake. And our Lord said concerning the daughter of the chief of the synagogue, The damsel is not dead, but sleeping a slumber. And concerning Lazarus, He said to His disciples:—Our friend Lazarus has fallen asleep; but I go to waken him. And the Apostle said:—We shall all sleep, but we shall not all be changed. And again he said:—Concerning those that sleep, be ye not grieved.

19. But it is right for us to be afraid of the second death, that which is full of weeping and gnashing of teeth, and of groanings and miseries, that which is situated in outer darkness. But blessed shall be the faithful and the righteous in that Resurrection, in which they expect to be awakened and to receive the good promises made them. But as for the wicked who are not faithful, in the Resurrection woe to them, because of that which is laid up for them! It would be better for them according to the faith which they possess, were they not to arise. For the servant, for whom his Lord is preparing stripes and bonds, while he is sleeping desires not to awake, for he knows that when the dawn shall have come and he shall awake, his Lord will scourge and bind him. But the good servant, to whom his Lord has promised gifts, looks expectantly for the time when dawn shall come and he shall receive presents from his Lord. And even though he is soundly sleeping, in his dream he sees something like what his Lord is about to give him, whatsoever He has promised him, and he rejoices in his dream, and exults, and is gladdened. As for the wicked, his sleep is not pleasant to him, for he imagines that lo! the dawn has come for him, and his heart is broken in his dream. But the righteous sleep, and their slumber is pleasant to them, in the day-time and the night-time, and they take no thought of all that long night, and like one hour is it accounted in their eyes. Then in the watch of the dawn they awake with joy. But as for the wicked, their sleep lies heavy upon them, and they are like a man who is laid low by a great and deep fever, and tosses on his couch hither and thither, and he is terrified the whole night long, which lengthens itself out for him, and he fears the dawn when his Lord will condemn him.

20. But our faith thus teaches, that when men fall asleep, they sleep this slumber without knowing good from evil. And the righteous look not forward to their promises, nor do the wicked look forward to their sentence of punishment, until the Judge come and separate those whose place is at His right hand from those whose place is at His left. And be thou instructed by that which is written, that when the Judge shall sit, and the books be opened before Him and the good and evil deeds recited, then they that have wrought good works shall receive good rewards from Him Who is good; and they that have done evil deeds shall receive evil penalties from the just Judge. For towards the good, He changes not His nature; and He proves Himself just because He justly condemns many. But towards the evil He changes His nature, in that world where grace is lost in justice; and He proves Himself just to all. And grace will not be joined with justice towards them. Like as grace avails not (to remedy) detriment, so justice (avails not to assist) grace. For grace is far from the judge, but justice urges the judge. If grace be nigh to any one, let him turn himself

towards it, and not deliver himself into the hands of justice, lest it condemn him, exacting for his shortcomings the penalty at his hands. And if grace be far from any one, justice will bring him to the trial, and by it he will be condemned, and go away to the torment.

21. But hear, my beloved, this proof that retribution shall take place at the end. For when the Shepherd divides His flock and sets some on His right hand and some on His left, until He shall have acknowledged the service of the good, then He will cause them to inherit the kingdom; and until He shall have rebuked the evil and they are condemned, then He will send them to the torment. And as to them that sent messengers after the King, saying, This man shall not be king over us, when He shall receive the kingdom and return, then His adversaries shall be slain before Him. And the labourers who hastened and were wearied in the vineyard, shall not receive the reward till the labour shall cease. And the traders who received the money, when the Lord of the money shall come, then shall He exact the usury. And the virgins who, while waiting for the bridegroom, slumbered and slept because He delayed to come, when they shall hear the cry, then they shall awake and trim their lamps; and they that are wise shall enter in; and the foolish shall be shut out. And they who were before us in entering the faith, without us shall not be made perfect.

22. From all these things, understand thou, my beloved, as it has been made certain for thee, that as yet no one has received his reward. For the righteous have not inherited the kingdom, nor have the wicked gone into torment. The Shepherd has not as yet divided His flock. And lo! the workmen enter into the vineyard, and as yet have not received the reward. And lo! the merchants are trading with the money. And as yet their Lord has not come to take the account. And the King has gone to receive the Kingdom, but as yet He has not returned the second time. And those virgins that are waiting the bridegroom are sleeping up to the present time, and are awaiting the cry when they will awake. And the former men who toiled in the faith until the last men shall come, shall not be made perfect.

23. But they who are babes in understanding say:—"If no one has received his reward, why did the Apostle say, When we shall depart from the body, we shall be present with the Lord?" But recollect, my beloved, that I instructed thee concerning this matter in the Demonstration concerning Solitaries, that the spirit which the righteous receive, according to its heavenly nature, goes to our Lord until the time of the Resurrection, when it shall come to put on the body in which it dwelt. And at every time it has the memory of this in the presence of God, and looks eagerly for the Resurrection of that body in which it dwelt, as the Prophet Isaiah said about the Church of the Gentiles:—They

that make mention of thee shall be faithful and stand before the Lord, and thou shalt not give them rest. But as to the wicked, they have none to make mention of them before the Lord, because the Holy Spirit is far removed from them, because they are animal, and are buried after the manner of animals.

24. And again, (the followers of) doctrines, which are instruments of the Evil One, are offended by the word which our Lord spake, No one has ascended up to heaven but He Who came down from heaven, the Son of Man, Who was in heaven. And they say, "Lo! our Lord testified that no earthly body has ascended to heaven." In their ignorance they cannot apprehend the force of this. For when our Lord instructed Nicodemus, he did not apprehend the force of the saying. Then our Lord said to him:—No one has ascended into heaven, so as to come down and relate to you whatsoever is there. For if I have spoken unto you of those things that are in the earth, and ye believe not, how shall ye believe if I shall speak unto you of those things which are in heaven? For lo! no other witness besides Me has come down from thence, to bear witness concerning those things which are in heaven, so that ye should believe. For Elijah went up thither, but he came not down along with Me to bear witness, that the testimony of two might be sure."

25. But as for thee, my beloved, have no doubt as to the Resurrection of the dead. For the living mouth (of God) testifies:—I cause to die and I make alive. And both of them proceeded out of one mouth. And as we are sure that He causes to die, and we see it; so also it is sure and worthy of belief, that He makes alive. And from all that I have explained to thee, receive and believe that in the day of the Resurrection thy body shall arise in its entirety, and thou shalt receive from our Lord the reward of thy faith, and in all that thou hast believed, thou shalt rejoice and be made glad.

Demonstration X

Of Pastors

1. Pastors are set over the flock, and give the sheep the food of life. Whosoever is watchful, and toils in behalf of his sheep, is careful for his flock, and is the disciple of our Good Shepherd, who gave Himself in behalf of His sheep. And whosoever brings not back his flock carefully, is likened to the hireling who has no care for the sheep. Be ye like, O Pastors, to those righteous Pastors of old. Jacob fed the sheep of Laban, and guarded them and toiled and was watchful, and so received the reward. For Jacob said to Laban:—Lo! twenty years am I with thee. Thy sheep and thy flocks I have not robbed and the males of thy sheep I have not eaten. That which was broken I did not bring unto thee, but thou required it at my hands! In the daytime the heat devoured me and the cold by night. My sleep departed from my eyes. Observe, ye Pastors, that Pastor, how he cared for his flock. He used to watch in the night-time to guard it and was vigilant; and he used to toil in the daytime to feed it. As Jacob was a pastor, so Joseph was a pastor and his brethren were pastors. Moses was a pastor, and David also was a pastor. So Amos was a pastor. These all were pastors who fed the sheep and led them well.

2. Now, why, my beloved, did these pastors first feed the sheep, and were then chosen to be pastors of men? Clearly that they might learn how a pastor cares for his sheep, and is watchful and toils in behalf of his sheep. And when they had learned the manners of pastors, they were chosen for the pastoral office. Jacob fed the sheep of Laban and toiled and was vigilant and led them well; and then he tended and guided well his sons, and taught them the pattern of pastoral work. And Joseph used to tend the sheep along with his brethren; and in Egypt he became guide to a numerous people, and led them back, as a good pastor does his flock. Moses fed the sheep of Jethro his father-in-law, and he was chosen from (tending) the sheep to tend his people, and as a good pastor he guided them. Moses bore his staff upon his shoulder, and went in

front of his people that he was leading, and tended them for forty years; and he was vigilant and toiled on behalf of his sheep, a diligent and good pastor. When his Lord wished to destroy them because of their sins, in that they worshipped the calf, Moses prayed and besought of his Lord and said:—Either pardon the people for their sins, or else blot me out from Thy book that Thou hast written. That is a most diligent pastor, who delivered over himself on behalf of his sheep. That is an excellent leader, who gave himself in behalf of his sheep. And that is a merciful father who cherished his children and reared them up. Moses the great and wise shepherd, who knew how to lead back the flock, taught Joshua the son of Nun, a man full of the spirit, who (afterwards) led the flock, even all the host of Israel. He destroyed kings and subdued the land, and gave them the land as a place of pasturage, and divided the resting-places and the sheepfolds to his sheep. Furthermore, David fed his father's sheep, and was taken from the sheep to tend his people. So he tended them in the integrity of his heart and by the skill of his hands he guided them. And when David numbered the flock of his sheep, wrath came upon them, and they began to be destroyed. Then David delivered himself over on behalf of his sheep, when he prayed, saying:—O Lord God, I have sinned in that I have numbered Israel. Let Thy hand be on me and on my father's house. These innocent sheep, in what have they sinned? So also all the diligent pastors used thus to give themselves on behalf of their sheep.

3. But those pastors who did not care for the sheep, those were hirelings who used to feed themselves alone. On this account the Prophet addresses them, saying to them:—O ye pastors who destroy and scatter the sheep of my pasture, hear the word of the Lord. Thus saith the Lord: Lo! I will visit My sheep as the pastor visits his flock in the day of the whirlwind, and I will require My sheep at your hands. O foolish pastors, with the wool of the sheep do ye clothe yourselves and the flesh of the fatlings do eat, and the sheep ye do not feed. That which was sick ye did not heal, and that which was broken ye did not bind. The weak ye did not strengthen, and the lost and the scattered ye did not gather together. The strong ones and the fatlings ye did guard, but with harshness ye subdued them. The good pastures ye yourselves graze upon, and what remains ye trample with your feet. The pleasant waters do ye drink, and whatever remains ye defile with your feet. And My sheep have eaten the trampled (herbage) which your feet have trampled, and they have drunk the waters which your feet have defiled. These are the greedy and base pastors and hirelings, who did not feed the sheep, or guide them well, or deliver them from the wolves. But when the Great Pastor, the chief of pastors, shall come, He will call and visit His sheep and will take knowledge of His flock. And He will

bring forward those pastors, and will exact an account from them, and will condemn them for their deeds. And those who fed the sheep well, them the Chief of Pastors will cause to rejoice and to inherit life and rest. O stupid and foolish pastor, to whose right hand and to whose right eye I committed my sheep. Because thou didst say concerning the sheep, let that which dieth, die, and let that which perisheth perish, and whatever is left, let them devour the flesh of one another; therefore, behold I will make blind thy right eye and I will wither up thy right arm. Thy eye which regarded a bribe shall be blinded, and thy hand which did not rule in righteousness shall waste away. And as for you, my sheep, the sheep of my pasture, ye are men; but I am the Lord your God. Behold henceforth will feed you in a good and rich pasture.

4. The good shepherd giveth himself for the sake of his sheep. And again He said:—I have other sheep and I must bring them also hither. And the whole flock shall be one, and one shepherd, and My Father because of this loveth Me; that I give Myself for the sake of the sheep. And again He said;—I am the door of the sheep. Every one that entereth by Me shall live and shall go in and go out and find pasture. O ye pastors, be ye made like unto that diligent pastor, the chief of the whole flock, who cared so greatly for his flock. He brought nigh those that were afar off. He brought back the wanderers. He visited the sick. He strengthened the weak. He bound up the broken. He guarded the fatlings. He gave himself up for the sake of the sheep. He chose and instructed excellent leaders, and committed the sheep into their hands, and gave them authority over all his flock. For He said to Simon Cephas:—Feed My sheep and My lambs and My ewes. So Simon fed His sheep; and he fulfilled his time and handed over the flock to you, and departed. Do ye also feed and guide them well. For the pastor who cares for his sheep engages in no other pursuit along with that. He does not make a vineyard, nor plant gardens, nor does he fall into the troubles of this world. Never have we seen a pastor who left his sheep in the wilderness and became a merchant, or one who left his flock to wander and became a husbandman. But if he deserts his flock and does these things he thereby hands over his flock to the wolves.

5. And remember, my beloved, that I wrote to thee concerning our fathers of old that they first learned the ways of tending sheep and in that received trial of carefulness, and then were chosen for the office of guides, that they might learn and observe how much the pastor cares for his flock, and as they used to guide the sheep carefully, so also might be perfected in this office of guidance. Thus Joseph was chosen from the sheep, to guide the Egyptians in the time of affliction. And Moses was chosen from the sheep, to guide his people and tend them. And David was taken from following the sheep, to

become king over Israel. And the Lord took Amos from following the sheep, and made him a prophet over his people. Elisha likewise was taken from behind the yoke, to become a prophet in Israel. Moses did not return to his sheep, nor did he leave his flock that was committed to him. David did not return to his father's sheep, but guided his people in the integrity of his heart. Amos did not turn back to feed his sheep, or to gather (the fruit of) trees, but he guided them and performed his office of prophecy. Elisha did not turn back to his yoke, but served Elijah and filled his place. And he who was for him as a shepherd, because he loved fields and merchandise and vineyards and oliveyards and tillage, did not wish to become his disciple; and (therefore) he did not commit the flock into his hand.

6. I beseech you, ye pastors, that ye set not over the flock, leaders who are foolish and stupid, covetous also and lovers of possessions. Every one who feeds the flock shall eat of their milk. And every one who guides the yoke shall be ministered to from his labour. The priests have a right to partake of the altar, and the Levites shall receive their tithes. Whoever eats of the milk, let his heart be upon the flock; and let him that is ministered to from the labour of his yoke, take heed to his tillage. And let the priests who partake of the altar serve the altar with honour. And as for the Levites who receive the tithes, they have no portion in Israel. O pastors, disciples of our great Pastor, be ye not like hirelings; because the hireling cares not for the sheep. Be ye like our Sweet Pastor, Whose life was not dearer to Him than His sheep. Rear up the youths and bring up the maidens; and love the lambs and let them be reared in your bosoms; that when ye shall come to the Chief Pastor, ye may offer to Him all your sheep in completeness, and so He may give you what He has promised: Where I am, ye also shall be. These things, brief as they are, will be sufficient for the good pastors and leaders.

7. Above, my beloved, I have written to remind thee of the character that becomes the whole flock. And in this discourse I have written to thee about the pastors, the guides of the flock. These reminders I have written to thee, beloved, as thou didst ask of me in thy dear letter.

8. The Steward brought me into the King's treasury and showed me there many precious things; and when I saw them my mind was captivated with the great treasury. And as I looked upon it, it dazzled my eyes, and took captive my thoughts, and caused my reflections to wander in many ways. Whosoever receives thereof, is himself enriched, and enriches (others). It lies open and unguarded before all that seek it; and though many take from it there is no deficiency; and when they give of that which they have received, their own portion is greatly multiplied. They that receive freely let them give freely as

they have received. For (this treasure) cannot be sold for a price, because there is nothing equivalent to it. Moreover the treasure fails not; and they that receive it are not satiated. They drink, and are still eager; they eat, and are hungry. Whosoever is not thirsty, finds not ought to drink; whoever is not hungry, finds nothing to eat. The hunger for it satisfies many, and from the thirst for it flow forth water-springs. For the man who draws nigh to the fear of God is like the man who in his thirst draws near to the water-spring and drinks and is satisfied, and the fountain is not a whit diminished. And the land that needs to drink in water, drinks of the fountain, but its waters fail not. And when the land drinks, it needs again to drink, and the spring is not lessened by its flowing. So is the knowledge of God. Though all men should receive of it, yet there would come no lack in it, nor can it be limited by the sons of flesh. He that takes from it, cannot take away all; and when he gives, he lacks nothing. When thou takest fire with a candle from a flame, though thou kindle many candles at it, yet the flame does not diminish when thou takest from it, nor does the candle fail, when it kindles many. One man cannot receive all the King's treasure, nor when a thirsty man drinks of the fountain, do its waters fill. When a man stands on a lofty mountain, his eye does not (equally) comprehend the near and the distant; nor, when he stands and counts the stars of heaven, can he set limits to the hosts of the heavens. So when he draws nigh unto the fear of God, he cannot attain to the whole of it; and when he receives much that is precious, it does not seem to be diminished; and when he gives of that which he has received, it is not exhausted, nor has it come to an end for him. And remember, my beloved, what I wrote to thee, in the first discourse, about faith, that whoever has freely received ought to give freely as he has received, as our Lord said:—Freely ye have received, freely give. For whosoever keeps back part of anything he has received, even that which he has obtained shall be taken away from him. Therefore, my beloved, as I have been able to obtain now from that treasure that fails not, I have sent unto thee from it. Yet though I have sent it to thee, it is all with me. For the treasure fails not, for it is the wisdom of God; and the steward is our Lord Jesus Christ, as He testified when He said:—All things have been committed to Me by My Father. And while He is the steward of the wisdom, again, as the Apostle said:—Christ is the power of God and His wisdom. This wisdom is imparted to many, yet nothing is lacking, as I explained to thee above; the Prophets received of the spirit of Christ, yet Christ was not a whit diminished.

9. Ten treatises have I written unto thee, my beloved. Whatsoever thou hast asked of me, I have explained to thee without (receiving) ought from thee. And that which thou enquiredst not of me, I have given unto thee. I have

asked thy name and written unto thee. I have asked of myself thy question, and I have answered thee as I was able, for thy persuasion. Whatsoever I have written unto thee, meditate in these things at every time; and labour to read those books which are read in the church of God. These ten little books that I have written for thee, they borrow one from another, and depend one upon another. Separate them not one from another. From Olaph to Yud I have written for thee, each letter after its fellow. Read thou and learn thou and the brethren, the monks, and the faithful, they from whom mocking is far removed; as I wrote unto thee above. And remember that which I pointed out to thee, that I have not brought these matters to an end, but short of the end. Nor are these things sufficient; but hear thou these things from me without wrangling, and enquire concerning them with brethren who are apt for persuasion. Whatsoever thou hearest that assuredly edifies, receive; and whatever builds up strange doctrines, overthrow and utterly demolish. For wrangling cannot edify. But I, my beloved, as a stonecutter have brought stones for the building, and let wise architects carve them out and lay them in the building; and all the labourers that toil in the building shall receive reward from the Lord of the house.

Demonstration XVII

Of Christ the Son of God

1. (This is) a reply against the Jews, who blaspheme the people gathered from among the Gentiles; for they say thus, "Ye worship and serve a man who was begotten, a son of man who was crucified, and ye call a son of men, God. And though God has no son, ye say concerning this crucified Jesus, that He is the Son of God." And they bring forward as an argument, that God said:—"I am God and there is none else beside Me." And again he said:—"Thou shalt not worship another God." Therefore, (say they), ye are opposing God in that ye call a man, God.

2. Concerning these things, my beloved, so far as I, in my insignificance, can comprehend, I will instruct thee about them, that while we grant to them that He is man, and (while) we at the same time honour Him and call Him God and Lord, yet it is not in any novel fashion, that we have so called Him, nor that we have applied to Him a novel name, which they themselves did not employ. Yet it is a sure thing with us, that Jesus our Lord is God, the Son of God, and the King, the King's Son, Light of light, Creator and Counsellor, and Guide, and the Way, and Redeemer, and Shepherd, Gatherer, and the Door, and the Pearl, and the Lamp; and by many (such) names is He surnamed. But we shall leave aside all (the rest) of them, and prove concerning Him, that He Who came from God is the Son of God, and (is) God.

3. For the venerated name of Godhead has been applied also to righteous men, and they have been held worthy to be called by it. And the men with whom God was well pleased, them He called, My sons, and My friends. When He chose Moses His friend and His beloved and made him chief and teacher and priest unto his people he called him God. For He said to him:—I have made thee a God unto Pharaoh. And He gave him His priest for a prophet, And Aaron thy brother shall speak for thee unto Pharaoh, and thou shalt be unto him as a God, and he shall be unto thee an interpreter. Thus not alone to

the evil Pharaoh did He make Moses God, but also unto Aaron, the holy priest, He made Moses God.

4. Again, hear concerning the title Son of God, by which we have called Him. They say that "though God has no son, ye make that crucified Jesus, the firstborn son of God." Yet He called Israel "My first-born," when He sent to Pharaoh through Moses and said to him, Israel is My first-born; I have said unto thee, let My Son go to serve Me, and if thou art not willing to let (him) go, lo! I will slay thy son, thy firstborn. And also through the Prophet He testified concerning this, and reproved them and said to the people, Out of Egypt have I called My son. As I called them, so they went and worshipped Baal and offered incense to the graven images. And Isaiah said concerning them, Children have I reared and brought up, and they have rebelled against Me. And again it is written, Ye are the children of the Lord your God. And about Solomon He said, He shall be to Me a son, and I will be to him a Father. So also we call the Christ, the Son of God, for through Him we have gained the knowledge of God; even as He called Israel My firstborn son, and as He said concerning Solomon, He shall be to Me a son. And we call Him God, even as He surnamed Moses by His own Name. And also David said concerning them:—Ye are Gods and children of the Highest, all of you. And when they amended not themselves, therefore He said concerning them:—As men shall ye die, and as one of the princes shall ye fall.

5. For the name of Divinity is given for the highest honour in the world, and with whomsoever God is well pleased, He applies it to him. But however, the names of God are many and are venerable, as He delivered His names to Moses, saying to him:—I am the God of your fathers, the God of Abraham and the God of Isaac and the God of Jacob. This is My Name for ever, and this is My memorial unto generations. And He called His name Ahiyah ashar Ahiyah, El Shaddai and Adonai Sabaoth. By these names is God called. The great and honourable name of Godhead He withheld not from His righteous ones; even as, though He is the great King, without grudging He applied the great and honourable name of Kingship to men who are His creatures.

6. For by the mouth of His prophet God called the heathen King Nebuchadnezzar, King of Kings. For Jeremiah said:—Every people and kingdom that shall not put his neck into the yoke of Nebuchadnezzar, King of Kings, My servant, with famine and with sword and with pestilence will I visit that people. Though He is the great King, He grudges not the name of Kingship to men. And (so), though He is the great God, yet He grudged not the name of Godhead to the sons of flesh. And though all fatherhood is His, He has called men also fathers. For He said to the congregation:—Instead of thy fathers,

shall be thy children. And though authority is His, He has given men authority one over another. And while worship is His unto honour, He has yet allowed it in the world, that one man should honour another. For even though a man should do worship before the wicked and the heathen and them that refuse grace, yet is he not censured by God. And concerning worship He commanded His people, Thou shalt not worship the sun or the moon or all the hosts of heaven; and also ye shall not desire to worship any creature that is upon the earth. Behold the grace and the love of our good Maker, that He did not grudge to men the name of Godhead and the name of worship, and the name of Kingship, and the name of authority; because He is the Father of the created things that are over the face of the world, and He has honoured and exalted and glorified men above all creatures. For with His holy hands He fashioned them; and of His Spirit He breathed into them, and a dwelling-place did He become unto them from of old. In them doth He abide and amongst them doth He walk. For He said through the prophet, I will dwell in them, and walk in them. Furthermore also the Prophet Jeremiah said:—Ye are the temple of the Lord, if ye make fair your ways and your deeds. And of old David said:—Thou, Lord, hast been a dwelling-place unto us for generations; before the mountains were conceived and before the earth travailed, and before the world was framed; from age to age Thou art God.

7. How dost thou understand this? For one prophet says:—Lord, Thou hast been our dwelling-place. And another said:—I will dwell in them and walk in them. First, He became to us a dwelling-place, and afterwards He dwelt and walked in us. For the wise both things are true and simple. For David says:—Thou, Lord, hast been our dwelling-place for generations, before the mountains were conceived and before the earth travailed, and before the world was framed. And thou knowest, my beloved, that all created things that are above and that are beneath were created first, and after them all, man. For when God determined to create the world with all its goodly things, first He conceived and fashioned man in His mind; and after that Adam was conceived in His thought, then He conceived the created things; as he said:—Before the mountains were conceived and the earth travailed; because man is older and more ancient in conception than the creatures, but in birth the creatures are older and more ancient than Adam. Adam was conceived and dwelt in the thought of God; and while in conception he (man) was held in His (God's) mind, He (God) by the word of His mouth created all the creatures. And when He had finished and adorned the world, when nothing was lacking in it, then He brought forth Adam from His thoughts, and fashioned man by His hands; and Adam saw the world completed. And He (God) gave him authority

over all that He had made, just as a man who has a son and desires to make for him a marriage feast, betroths to him a wife and builds for him a house, and prepares and adorns all that is needed for his son; then he makes the marriage feast and gives his son authority over his house. So after the conception of Adam, He brought him forth and gave him authority over all his creation. Concerning this the Prophet said:—Thou, Lord, hast been our habitation for generations, before the mountains were conceived, and before the earth travailed and before the world was framed. From age unto age Thou art the Lord. That no one should suppose that there is another God, either before or afterwards, he said:—From age and unto age, just as Isaiah said:—I am the first and I am the last. And after that God brought forth Adam from within His thought, He fashioned him, and breathed into him of His Spirit, and gave him the knowledge of discernment, that he might discern good from evil, and might know that God made him. And inasmuch as man knew his Maker, God was formed and conceived within his thought, and he became a temple for God his Maker, as it is written, Ye are the temple of God. And (so) He Himself said:—I will dwell in them and walk in them. But as for the sons of Adam, who do not recognise their Maker, He is not formed within them, and does not dwell in them, and is not conceived in their thought; but they are accounted before Him as the beasts, and as the rest of the creatures.

8. Now by these things the stubborn will be convinced, that it is nothing strange that we call Christ the Son of God. For behold, He (God) conceived all men and brought them forth from His thoughts. And they will be forced to own that the name of Godhead also belongs to Him (Christ), for He (God) associated the righteous also in the name of God. And as to this, that we worship Jesus through Whom we have known God, let them be ashamed, inasmuch as they fall down and worship and honour even the heathen of the unclean Gentiles, if they possess authority; and (for this) there is no blame. And this honour of worship God has given to the sons of Adam, that by it they might honour one another—especially those who excel and are worthy of honour amongst them. For if they worship, and honour with the name of worship, the heathen—those who in their heathen wickedness deny even the name of God—and yet do not worship them as their maker, as though they worshipped them alone, and so do not sin; how much more does it become us to worship and honour Jesus, Who converted our stubborn minds from all worship of vain error, and taught us to worship and serve and minister to the one God, our Father and our Maker. And (taught us) to know that the kings of the world call themselves Gods by the name of the great God, and are infidels and force men to infidelity, and men fall down and worship before

them and serve and honour them, like carven images and idols, yet the law never censured these, and there is no sin. As Daniel also used to do worship to Nebuchadnezzar, King of Babylon, the infidel and compeller to infidelity, and was not censured. Joseph also gave worship to Pharaoh, and it is not written that it was a sin for him. But as for us, we are certain that Jesus is God, the Son of God, and through Him we know His Father, and (have) all of us (turned away) from all other worship. Therefore it is impossible for us to repay Him Who bore these things for us. But by worship let us pay Him honour in return for His affliction that was on our behalf.

9. Furthermore, we must prove that this Jesus was beforehand promised from ancient times in the Prophets, and was called the Son of God. David said:—Thou art My Son; today have I begotten Thee. Again he said:—In the glories of holiness, from the womb, from of old, have I begotten thee, a child. And Isaiah said:—Unto us a child is born, unto us a Son is given, and His government was upon His shoulder, and His Name shall be called Wonderful, and Counsellor, and mighty God of the ages, and Prince of peace. And to the increase of His government and to His peace there is no end. Therefore tell me, O wise doctor of Israel, who is He that was born and whose name was called Child and Son and Wonderful and Counsellor, the mighty God of the ages, and Prince of peace, to the increase of whose government and to whose peace (he said), there is no end? For if we call Christ the Son of God, David taught us (this); and that we call Him God, this we learned from Isaiah. And His government was laid upon His shoulder; for He bare His cross, and went out from Jerusalem. And that He was born as a child, Isaiah again said:—Lo, the virgin shall conceive and bear; and His name shall be called Immanuel, which is, our God with us.

10. And if thou shouldest say that Christ has not yet come, I will grant this also to thy contentiousness. For it is written that when He shall come, the Gentiles shall expect Him. Lo! I, one of the Gentiles, have heard that Christ is to come. And when as yet He had not come, I beforehand have believed on Him; and through Him I worship the God of Israel. When He comes, will He then blame me because before His coming I beforehand believed on Him? But, thou fool, the prophets suffer thee not to say that Christ has not yet come; for Daniel confutes thee, saying:—After sixty-two weeks shall Messiah come and shall be slain. And in His coming shall the Holy City be laid waste, and her end shall be with a flood. And until the accomplishment of the things that are determined, shall she continue in desolation. Thou expectest and hopest that, at the coming of Christ, Israel shall be gathered together from all regions, and Jerusalem shall be built up and inhabited. But Daniel testifies that, when

Christ comes and is slain, Jerusalem shall be destroyed, and shall continue in desolation until the accomplishment of the things which are determined, forever. And concerning the suffering of Christ, David said:—They pierced my hands and my feet, and all my bones cried out. They gazed and looked upon me, and divided my garments amongst them, and upon my vesture did they cast the lot. And Isaiah said:—Lo! My servant shall be known and shall be revealed and shall be lifted up, so that many shall be astonished at Him. As for this man, His visage shall be marred more than that of man, and His aspect more than that of the sons of men. And he said:—He will purify many nations, and kings shall be amazed at Him. And he said in that passage:—He came up as a little child before Him, and as a root from the dry ground. And in the end of the passage he said:—He shall be slain for our sins; He shall be humiliated for our iniquity; the chastisement of our peace is upon Him, and by His bruises shall we be healed. By what wounds were men healed? David was not slain; for he died in a good old age, and was buried in Bethlehem. And if they should say that it is spoken of Saul, for Saul was killed in the mountains of Gilboa in the battle with the Philistines, and if they should say that they pierced his hands and his feet, when they fastened up his body on the wall of Bethshan; yet it does not fitly apply to Saul. When the limbs of Saul were pierced, his bones were not conscious of suffering, because he was dead. It was after Saul died, that they hanged his body and those of his sons on the wall of Bethshan. But when David said, They pierced my hands and my feet, and all my bones cried out, he said in the next verse:—O God, abide for my help, and deliver my soul from the sword. Now Christ was delivered from the sword, and ascended from out of Sheol, and revived and rose the third day, and so God abode for His help. But Saul called upon the Lord and He did not answer him; and he asked through the Prophets, but no answer was given to him. And he disguised himself and inquired by soothsayers, and learned from thence. He was worsted before the Philistines, and he slew himself with his own sword, when he saw that the battle had overcome him. Moreover in this passage David said:—I will declare Thy name unto my brethren, and in the midst of the congregation will I glorify Thee. How can these things apply to Saul? And again David said:—Thou didst not give Thy holy one to see corruption. But all these things fitly apply to Christ. When He came to them, they did not receive Him; but wickedly judged Him by false witness. And He was hung upon the tree by His hands, and they pierced His hands and His feet with the nails which they fastened in him; and all His bones cried out. And on that day a great prodigy happened. namely, that the light became dark in the middle of the day, as Zechariah prophesied, saying:—The day shall be known unto the

Lord. It shall not be daytime, and it shall not be night; and at the evening time there shall be light. Now what is the day that was distinguished by the prodigy, that it was neither daytime nor night, and that at the evening time there was light? Evidently the day on which they crucified Him, for in the midst of that day there came darkness, and at the evening time there was light. And again he said:—That day there shall be cold and frost.—As thou knowest, on that day on which they crucified Him, it was cold, and they had made them a fire to warm themselves when Simon came and stood with them. And again he said:—The spear shall arise against the shepherd, and against the man, My friend; and it shall smite the shepherd, and the sheep of his flock shall be scattered; and I will turn back My hand upon the pastor. And furthermore David said concerning His Passion:—For My meat they gave gall, and for My thirst did they give Me vinegar to drink.—Again he said in that passage:—They have persecuted Him Whom Thou hast smitten; and have added to the affliction of Him that was slain. For they added many (afflictions) to Him, much that was not written concerning Him, cursings and revilings, such as the Scripture could not reveal, for their revilings were hateful. But, however, the Lord was pleased to humiliate Him and afflict Him. And He was slain for our iniquity, and was humiliated for our sins, and was made sin in His own person.

11. We worship those mercies, and bow the knee before the Majesty of His Father, Who converted our worship to Him. We call Him God, just as Moses (was called God); and Firstborn, and Son, just as Israel (was called); and Jesus (Joshua), just as Joshua the son of Nun was so called; and Priest like Aaron, and King, like David; and great Prophet, like all the Prophets; and Shepherd, like the shepherds who tended and guided Israel. And so did He call children as He said:—Strange children shall hearken unto Me. And He has made us brothers unto Himself, He said:—I will declare Thy name unto My brethren. And we have become friends unto Him, as He said to His disciples:—I have called you friends, even as His Father called Abraham My friend. And He said unto us:—I am the good Shepherd, the Door, the Way, the Vine, the Sower, the Bridegroom, the Pearl, the Lamp, the Light, the King, God, Saviour, and Redeemer. And by many names is He surnamed.

12. This brief argument have I written unto thee, my beloved, that thou mayest make defence against the Jews, concerning this that they say, that God has no son, and concerning this that we call Him God, the Son of God, King, and Firstborn of all creatures.

Demonstration XXI

Of Persecution

1. I have heard a reproach, which has greatly vexed me. The unclean (the heathen) say, that this people, which is gathered together out of all nations, has no God. And thus say the impious:—"If they have a God, why does He not avenge His people?" And darkness more exceedingly has thickened upon me, because the Jews also reproach us, and magnify themselves over the children of our people. It happened one day, that a man, who is called wise amongst the Jews, questioned me, saying:—Jesus, Who is called your Teacher, wrote for you, that If there shall be in you faith like one grain of mustard, ye shall say to this mountain, Remove, and it shall remove from before you; and (ye shall say) even, Be lifted up and fall into the sea, and it shall obey you. So apparently there is in all your people not one wise man, whose prayer is heard, and who asks of God that your persecutors should cease from you. For clearly it is written for you in that passage, There is nothing which ye shall not be able to do.

2. And when I saw that he was blaspheming and speaking much against the Way (the Christian religion), my mind was disturbed, and I understood that he would not admit the interpretation of the words that he quoted to me. Then I also questioned him on sayings from the Law and from the Prophets, and said to him:—Do ye trust that even when ye are dispersed God is with you? And he professed to me, "God is with us, because that God said unto Israel:—Even in the lands of their enemies, I yet did not forsake them, nor did I make void My covenant with them." In answer I said to him:—"Right good is this that I have heard from thee, that God is with you. Against thy words will I also speak unto thee. For I said the Prophet said unto Israel, as from the mouth of God:—If thou shalt pass through the sea, I will be with thee, and the rivers shall not overflow thee; and if thou shalt walk upon fire, thou shalt not be burned, and the flame shall not search thee; because the Lord thy God is

with thee. Thus there is not one righteous and good and wise man out of all your people, who could pass through the sea and live and not be drowned; or (through) the river without its overflowing him; or who could walk over fire and see whether he would not be scorched and whether the flame would not burn him. And if thou shalt bring to me an explanation, I will not be persuaded by thee, just as thou also dost not accept from me the interpretation of the words as to which thou hast questioned me."

3. Furthermore I questioned him about another saying that is written in Ezekiel; namely, that he said to Jerusalem:—Sodom and her daughters shall be built up as of old, and thou and thy daughters shall become as of old. So he explained this saying to me, and began to make a defence, and said to me "As to this that God said to Jerusalem by the Prophet, Sodom and her daughters shall be built up as of old, and thou and thy daughters shall become as of old; this is the force of the passage, that Sodom and her daughters shall be in their place as of old, and shall be made subject to Israel; and Jerusalem and her daughters shall be in the splendour of royalty as of old." When I heard this defence from him, it was very contemptible in my eyes, and I said to him:—"Inasmuch as the words of the Prophet were said in wrath, is the whole passage wrathful, or is part of it wrathful and part of it gracious?" He answered:—"A wrathful passage is altogether wrath, and there is no peace in it." And I said to him:—"Since thou hast instructed me that there is no peace in that wrathful passage, hear without contention and blaspheme not, and I will instruct thee about this saying. For from the top to the bottom the whole passage is said in wrath. For he said to Jerusalem:—As I live, saith the Lord God, Sodom and her daughters did not do at all as thou and they daughters have done. And he said to her (Jerusalem):—Be abashed and accept thy shame, that thou hast overcome thy sisters in thy sins, and they are justified rather than thou. Since he says that Sodom and her daughters were justified rather than Jerusalem and her daughters, and that Jerusalem overcame Sodom in her sins, it is right that when Israel shall be gathered together, its seat should be in Sodom and Gomorrha. For their vine is of the vine of Sodom, and of the planting of Gomorrha. Their grapes are bitter and their clusters gall unto them. And Isaiah also calls them rulers of Sodom, and people of Gomorrha. For if Israel is gathered together, in Sodom and Gomorrha ought they to dwell with the rulers of Sodom and with the people of Gomorrha; and on the vine of Sodom and planting of Gomorrha to eat bitter grapes and gather clusters of gall; and to eat the eggs of the basilisk and to clothe themselves with spiders' webs, to be used with wild grapes of the vineyard, and to be turned into reprobate silver. And Sodom and her daughters, who were justified rather than Jerusalem, shall be

built up as of old. And Jerusalem, that surpassed Sodom in her sins, shall continue in her sins, and shall remain in desolation until the accomplishment of the things determined for ever.

4. And Ezekiel said:—This is the iniquity of Sodom and of her daughters, that they did not take by the hand the poor and needy; and when I saw these things in them, I overthrew them. And consider and see that, from the time that Sodom was overthrown until Jerusalem was built, there were eight hundred and ninety-six years. From the time that Abraham was informed by God through the Angel that at this time next year I will return to thee, and Sarah thy wife shall have a son, from that time till Jacob entered Egypt was a hundred and ninety-one years: and the children of Jacob were in Egypt two hundred and twenty-five years. So all the years from the time that Isaac was conceived and Sodom overthrown were four hundred and sixteen years, and from the Exodus of Israel from Egypt till the great edifice of Jerusalem was built up by Solomon, and the temple was built, there were four hundred and eighty years. Therefore all the years from the conception of Isaac and the overthrow of Sodom till the great building of Jerusalem, were eight hundred and ninety-six years. And from the great building of Jerusalem until the destruction of Jerusalem there were four hundred and twenty-five years. The sum of all the years from the time of the overthrow of Sodom until Jerusalem was laid waste, was one thousand three hundred and twenty-one. These are all the years that Sodom and her daughters were laid waste before Jerusalem. And she that was more just than Jerusalem is not yet inhabited. Therefore the whole sum of the years from the overthrow of Sodom till the six hundred and fifty-fifth year of the Kingdom of Alexander, the son of Philip of Macedon, is two thousand two hundred and seventy-six years. And from the time that Jerusalem was laid waste by the Babylonians until the present time is nine hundred and fifty-five years. And Jerusalem has been inhabited, after the Babylonians laid it waste, during those seventy weeks about which Daniel testified. Then it was laid waste in its last destruction by the Romans, and it shall not be inhabited again for ever, for it abideth in desolation until the accomplishment of the things determined. So then, all the years of the former and latter desolation of Jerusalem have been four hundred and sixty-five years, and when thou dost deduct from them the seventy years of Babylon, they have been three hundred and ninety-five years.

5. All this argument have I written to thee, because the Jews pride themselves, (saying), "It has been covenanted to us, that we shall be gathered." For if Sodom, whose iniquity was not so great as that of Jerusalem, is not as yet inhabited, and if we say thus, that it will not be restored for ever, how shall

Jerusalem be restored, whose iniquity is greater than that of Sodom and her daughters? As for Sodom God has not had mercy on her for two thousand two hundred and seventy-six years; and shall we say that He will have mercy on Jerusalem? For up to the present there are but three hundred and ninety-five years from the day that she was laid waste, according to the calculation that has been written above. But as to this that he said, Sodom and her daughters shall be possessed as of old, and with regard to Jerusalem he said, Thou and thy daughters shall become as of old, this is the force of the passage; that they shall not be inhabited for ever; for the Lord also thus cursed the land against which He was wroth:—It shall not be sown, nor shall it produce, nor shall any herb spring up in it, but it shall be like Sodom and Gomorrha, against which the Lord was wroth and towards which He was not appeased. Therefore be sure, my hearer, that Sodom and her daughters shall not be inhabited for ever; but they shall be as of old, namely, as in that time when they were not as yet inhabited, and as in the time when the Lord was wroth with them and was not appeased towards them. And Jerusalem and her daughters shall be as of old, (that is) as in the former time when the mountain of the Amorites lay in desolation, whereon Abraham built the altar, when he bound upon it Isaac his son; and as it was desolate when David bought the threshing-floor from Araunah the Jebusite, and built there the altar. For consider and see that this mountain whereon Abraham offered his son is the mountain of Jebus, which is Jerusalem. And this place of the threshing-floor that David bought of Araunah is that whereon the Temple was built. Thus Jerusalem shall be in desolation as of old. And consider that when Ezekiel prophesied this passage, Jerusalem still was sitting in her greatness, and those who were in her were rebelling against the King of Babylon. And that which the Prophet spoke, he said in wrath and reproach against Jerusalem.

6. Consider and observe, my hearer, that if God had given a hope to Sodom and to her fellows, He would not have overthrown them with fire and brimstone, the sign of the last day of the world, but would have delivered them over to one of the kingdoms to be chastised. As it is written that when Jeremiah caused the nations and kingdoms to drink the cup of wrath, he said concerning each one of the cities, that after they shall drink the cup, I will turn back the captivity of Elam, of Tyre, of Zidon, of the children of Ammon, and of Moab, and of Edom. Concerning each one of these kingdoms he said:—In the last days I well turn back her captivity. Now we see that Tyre was inhabited, and was opulent after she had wandered seventy years, and after she had received the reward of her harlotries and after she had committed fornication with all kingdoms. And she took the harp, and played it sweetly, and multi-

plied her music. And also the region of Elam is inhabited and opulent. And with regard to Babylon Jeremiah said:—Babylon shall fall, and shall not rise. And lo! unto this day does it continue in desolation, and will do so for ever. And also about Jerusalem he said:—The virgin of Israel shall fall, and shall not rise again. She is forsaken upon the ground and there is none to raise her up. For if the prophecy is true which Jeremiah spoke about Babylon, also that about Jerusalem is true and worthy of faith. And Isaiah said unto Jerusalem:—I will not again be wroth with thee, nor will I reprove thee. Of a truth He will not again be wroth with her, nor will He reprove her for ever; for that which is in desolation He will not reprove, nor will she provoke him to wrath.

7. As to those that reproach us (saying):—"Ye are persecuted and are not delivered," let them be ashamed themselves, that at every time they have been persecuted, even for many years before they were delivered. They were made to serve in Egypt two hundred and twenty-five years. And the Midianites made Israel serve in the days of Barak and Deborah. The Moabites ruled over them in the days of Ehud; the Ammonites in the days of Jephthah; the Philistines in the days of Samson, and also in the days of Eli and of Samuel the Prophet; the Edomites in the days of Ahab; the Assyrians in the days of Hezekiah. The king of Babylon uprooted them from their place and dispersed them; and after he had tried and persecuted them much, they did not amend, as He said to them:—In vain have I smitten your sons, for they did not accept chastisement. And again He said:—I have cut off the Prophets, and slain them by the word of My mouth. And to Jerusalem He said:—By afflictions and scourges be instructed, O Jerusalem, lest thy life depart from thee. But they forsook Him, and worshipped idols, as Jeremiah said concerning them:—Go to the distant isles, and send to Kedar, and consider well and see, whether there has been (anything) like this, whether the nations change their gods, those that are no gods. But My people has changed My honour for that which is not profitable. Be astonished, ye heavens, at this; and quake and fear greatly, saith the Lord; because My people have done two wickednesses; they have abandoned Me, the fountain of the water of life, and they have gone and dug for themselves cisterns, broken cisterns which cannot hold water. For the broken cisterns are the fear of images and idols. And He calls the heavens to astonishment, because they worshipped the hosts of the heavens. And the heavens shall receive as a penalty, that they shall be rolled up as a scroll, and all the host of them shall fall down.

8. All this discourse that I have written unto thee, my beloved, from the beginning, was because the Jew reproached the children of our people; but now, as far as I can comprehend, I will instruct thee about the persecuted, that

they have received a great reward, while the persecutors have come to scorn and contempt.

9. Jacob was persecuted, and Esau was a persecutor. Jacob received the blessings and the birthright, while Esau was cast out from both. Joseph was persecuted, and his brothers were persecutors; Joseph was exalted and his persecutors bowed down before him, and so his dreams and his visions were fulfilled. Joseph who was persecuted was a type of the persecuted Jesus. His father clothed Joseph in a tunic of divers colours; and His Father clothed Jesus with a body (taken) from the Virgin. His father loved Joseph more than his brethren, and Jesus is the dear and beloved one of His Father. Joseph saw visions and dreamed dreams; Jesus fulfilled the visions and the Prophets. Joseph was a shepherd with his brethren; and Jesus is the Chief of Shepherds. When his father sent Joseph to visit his brethren, they saw him coming and plotted to kill him; and when His Father sent Jesus to visit His brethren, they said:—This is the heir; come, let us kill him. His brethren cast Joseph into the pit; and His brethren brought down Jesus into the abode of the dead. Joseph ascended from the pit and Jesus arose from the abode of the dead. Joseph, after he arose from the pit, had authority over his brethren; and after Jesus arose from the abode of the dead, His Father gave Him a great and excellent name, that His brethren should serve Him, and His enemies be put beneath His feet. After that Joseph was made known to his brethren, they were abashed and feared and were amazed at his greatness; and when Jesus shall come at the last time, when He shall be revealed in His Majesty, His brethren will be abashed and fear and be dismayed before Him, because they crucified Him. Moreover, Joseph, by the counsel of Judah, was sold into Egypt; and Jesus, by the hands of Judas Iscariot, was delivered over to the Jews. When they sold Joseph, he answered nothing to his brethren; Jesus also spake not and gave no answer to the judges who judged Him. His master wrongfully delivered over Joseph to the prison; and His countrymen wrongfully condemned Jesus. Joseph delivered over his two garments, one into the hand of his brethren, and the other into the hand of his master's wife; and Jesus delivered over His garments and divided them between the soldiers. Joseph, when thirty years old, stood before Pharaoh and became lord of Egypt; and Jesus, when about thirty years old, came to the Jordan to be baptized, and received the spirit, and went forth to preach. Joseph nourished Egypt with bread; and Jesus nourished the whole world with the bread of life. Joseph took to wife the daughter of the wicked and unclean priest; and Jesus espoused to Himself the Church (taken) from the unclean Gentiles. Joseph died and was buried in Egypt; and Jesus died and was buried in Jerusalem. Joseph's bones his brethren brought up from Egypt; and

Jesus His Father raised from the abode of the dead, and took up His Body with Him to heaven uncorrupted.

10. Moses also was persecuted, as Jesus was persecuted. When Moses was born, they concealed him that he might not be slain by his persecutors. When Jesus was born they carried Him off in flight into Egypt that Herod, His persecutor, might not slay Him. In the days when Moses was born, children used to be drowned in the river; and at the birth of Jesus the children of Bethlehem and in its borders were slain. To Moses God said:—The men are dead who were seeking thy life; and to Joseph the angel said in Egypt:—Arise, take up the child, and go into the land of Israel, for they are dead who were seeking the life of the child to take it away. Moses brought out his people from the service of Pharaoh; and Jesus delivered all nations from the service of Satan. Moses grew up in Pharaoh's house; and Jesus grew up in Egypt when Joseph brought Him there in flight. Miriam stood on the edge of the river when Moses was floating in the water; and Mary bare Jesus, after the Angel Gabriel had made the annunciation to her. When Moses sacrificed the lamb, the firstborn of Egypt were slain; and when they crucified Jesus the true Lamb, the people who slew Him perished through His slaying. Moses brought down manna for his people; and Jesus gave His Body to the nations. Moses sweetened the bitter waters by the wood; and Jesus sweetened our bitterness by His cross, by the wood of the tree of His crucifixion. Moses brought down the Law to his people; and Jesus gave His covenants to the nations. Moses conquered Amalek by the spreading out of his hands; and Jesus conquered Satan by the sign of His cross. Moses brought out water from the rock for his people; and Jesus sent Simon Cephas (the rock) to carry His doctrine among the nations. Moses lifted up the veil from his face and spake with God; and Jesus lifted up the veil from the face of the nations, that they might hear and receive His doctrine. Moses laid his hand upon his messengers (apostles), and they received priesthood; and Jesus laid His hand upon His apostles, and they received the Holy Spirit. Moses ascended the mountain and died there; and Jesus ascended into heaven and took his seat at the right hand of His Father.

11. Also Joshua the son of Nun was persecuted as Jesus our Redeemer was persecuted. Joshua the son of Nun was persecuted by the unclean nations; and Jesus our Redeemer was persecuted by the foolish people. Joshua the son of Nun took away the inheritance from his persecutors and gave it to his people; and Jesus our Redeemer took away the inheritance from His persecutors and gave it to strange nations. Joshua the son of Nun caused the sun to stand still in the heavens, and took vengeance on the nations his persecutors; and Jesus our Redeemer caused the sun to set in the midst of the day, that the persecut-

ing people which crucified Him might be ashamed. Joshua the son of Nun divided the inheritance unto his people; and Jesus our Redeemer has promised to give to the nations the land of life. Joshua the son of Nun caused Rahab the harlot to live; and Jesus our Redeemer gathered together and gave life to the Church, though polluted by the harlotry (of idolatry). Joshua the son of Nun on the seventh day overthrew and cast down the walls of Jericho; and Jesus our Redeemer, on His seventh day, on the Sabbath of the rest of God, this world shall be dissolved and fall. Joshua the son of Nun stoned Achor, because he stole of the accursed thing; and Jesus our Redeemer separated Judas from the disciples, His friends, because he stole of the money of the poor. Joshua the son of Nun, when he was dying, laid down a testimony among his people; and Jesus our Redeemer, when He was taken up, laid down a testimony among His apostles.

12. Also Jephthah was persecuted, as Jesus was persecuted. Jephthah, his brethren drove out from the house of his father; and Jesus, His brethren drove out and lifted up and crucified. Jephthah though persecuted arose as leader to his people; Jesus though persecuted arose and became King of the Nations. Jephthah vowed a vow and offered up his firstborn daughter as a sacrifice; and Jesus was lifted up as a sacrifice to his Father for all the Gentiles.

13. Also David was persecuted, as Jesus was persecuted. David was anointed by Samuel to be king instead of Saul who had sinned; and Jesus was anointed by John to be High Priest instead of the priests, the ministers of the Law. David was persecuted after his anointing; and Jesus was persecuted after His anointing. David reigned first over one tribe only, and afterwards over all Israel; and Jesus reigned from the beginning over the few who believed on Him, and in the end He will reign over all the world. Samuel anointed David when he was thirty years old; and Jesus when about thirty years old received the imposition of the hand from John. David wedded two daughters of the king; and Jesus wedded two daughters of kings, the congregation of the People and the congregation of the Gentiles. David repaid good to Saul his enemy; and Jesus taught, Pray for your enemies. David was the heart of God; and Jesus was the Son of God. David received the kingdom of Saul his persecutor; and Jesus received the kingdom of Israel His persecutor. David wept with dirges over Saul his enemy when he died; and Jesus wept over Jerusalem, His persecutor, which was to be laid waste. David handed over the kingdom to Solomon, and was gathered to his people; and Jesus handed over the keys to Simon, and ascended and returned to Him who sent Him. For David's sake, sins were forgiven to his posterity; and for Jesus' sake sins are forgiven to the nations.

14. Elijah also was persecuted as Jesus was persecuted. Jezebel the murderess persecuted Elijah; and the persecuting and murderous congregation persecuted Jesus. Elijah restrained the heavens from rain because of the sins of Israel; and Jesus by His coming restrained the Spirit from the prophets, because of the sins of the people. Elijah destroyed the servants of Baal; and Jesus trampled upon Satan and his hosts. Elijah raised to life the son of the widow; and Jesus raised to life the son of the widow, as well as Lazarus and the daughter of the ruler of the Synagogue. Elijah sustained the widow with a little bread; and Jesus satisfied thousands with a little bread. Elijah was taken up in a chariot to heaven; and our Redeemer ascended and took His seat on the right hand of His Father. Elisha received the spirit of Elijah; and Jesus breathed upon the faces of His Apostles.

15. Also Elisha was persecuted as Jesus was persecuted. Elisha was persecuted by the son of Ahab, the son of the murderer; and Jesus was persecuted by the murderous people. Elisha prophesied, and there came about abundance in Samaria; and Jesus said:—Whosoever eateth of My body and drinketh of My blood shall live for ever. Elisha satisfied a hundred men with a little bread; and Jesus satisfied four thousand men, besides women and children, with five loaves. Elisha made oil out of water; and Jesus made wine out of water. Elisha delivered the widow from her creditor; and Jesus delivered the indebted nations. Elisha made the iron to swim and the wood to sink; and Jesus raised up that which was sunk in us, and sank that which was light. A dead man (laid) upon the bones of Elisha recovered life; and all the nations, who were dead in their sins, were cast upon the bones of Jesus and recovered life.

16. Hezekiah also was persecuted as Jesus was persecuted. Hezekiah was persecuted, and was reproached by Sennacherib his enemy; Jesus also was reproached by the foolish people. Hezekiah prayed and overcame his adversary; and by the crucifixion of Jesus was our Adversary overcome. Hezekiah was king of all Israel; and Jesus is King of all the nations. Because Hezekiah was sick, the sun turned backwards; and because Jesus suffered, the sun was darkened from its light. The enemies of Hezekiah became dead corpses; and Jesus, His enemies shall be cast down beneath His feet. Hezekiah was of the family of the house of David; and Jesus was, in the flesh, the son of David. Hezekiah said:—Peace and truth shall be in my days; and Jesus said to His disciples:—My peace I leave with you. Hezekiah prayed, and was healed of his sickness; Jesus prayed, and arose from the abode of the dead. Hezekiah after he arose from his sickness added to his years; and Jesus after His Resurrection received great glory. Hezekiah, after the prolongation of his life, death was given do-

minion over him; but Jesus, after that He rose, death shall not again have dominion over Him for ever.

17. Josiah also was persecuted as Jesus was persecuted. Josiah was persecuted, and Pharaoh the Lame slew Him; and Jesus was persecuted, and the people that were made lame by their sins slew Him. Josiah cleansed the land of Israel from uncleanness; and Jesus cleansed and caused to pass away uncleanness from all the earth. Josiah hallowed and glorified the name of his God; and Jesus said:—I have glorified and will glorify (His Name). Josiah because of the iniquity of Israel rent his clothes; and Jesus because of the iniquity of the people rent the vail of the Holy Temple. Josiah said:—Great is the wrath that shall come upon this people; and Jesus said:—There shall come wrath upon this people, and they shall fall by the edge of the sword. Josiah cast out uncleanness from the Holy Temple; and Jesus cast out the unclean traders from His Father's house. For Josiah the daughters of Israel mourned and wailed, as Jeremiah said:—O daughters of Israel, weep for Josiah; and over Jesus did the daughters of Israel weep and mourn, as Zechariah said:—The land shall mourn, families over families.

18. Daniel also was persecuted as Jesus was persecuted. Daniel was persecuted by the Chaldeans, the congregation of heathen men; Jesus also the Jews, the congregation of wicked men, persecuted. Daniel the Chaldeans accused; and Jesus the Jews accused before the governor. Daniel they cast into the pit of lions, and he was delivered and came up out of its midst uninjured; and Jesus they sent down into the pit of the abode of the dead, and He ascended, and death had not dominion over him. Concerning Daniel they expected that when he had fallen into the pit he would not come up again; and concerning Jesus they said, Since He has fallen, He shall not rise again. From (harming) Daniel the mouth of the ravenous and destructive lions was closed; and from (harming) Jesus was closed the mouth of death, (though) ravenous and destructive of (living) forms. They sealed the pit of Daniel, and guarded it with diligence; and the grave of Jesus did they guard with diligence, as they said, Set guards to watch al the tomb. When Daniel came up, his accusers were ashamed; and when Jesus rose, all they who had crucified Him were ashamed. The King who judged Daniel was greatly grieved at the wickedness of his accusers the Chaldeans; and Pilate who judged Jesus was greatly grieved because he knew that for malice the Jews were accusing Him. At the prayer of Daniel, the captivity of his people went up from Babylon; and Jesus by His prayer turned back the captivity of all the nations, Daniel interpreted the visions and dreams of Nebuchadnezzar; and Jesus explained and interpreted the visions of the Law and the Prophets. When Daniel explained the vision of

Belteshazzar, he received authority over the third part of the kingdom; and when Jesus fulfilled the visions and the Prophets, His Father delivered unto Him all authority in heaven and in earth. Daniel saw wonders and uttered secrets; and Jesus revealed secrets and fulfilled what is written. Daniel was led away among the hostages in behalf of his people; and the body of Jesus was a hostage in behalf of all nations. For Daniel's sake the wrath of the King was appeased from the Chaldeans, so that they were not slain; and for Jesus' sake the wrath of His Father was appeased from all nations, so that they were not slain and died not because of their sins. Daniel besought of the king, and he gave his brethren authority over the affairs of the province of Babylon; and Jesus besought of God, and He gave His brethren, His disciples, authority over Satan and his host. Daniel said concerning Jerusalem, that until the things determined, she should remain in desolation; and Jesus said concerning Jerusalem, There shall not be left in her stone upon stone, because she knew not the day of her greatness. Daniel foresaw the weeks that should remain over for his people; and Jesus came and fulfilled them.

19. Hananiah also and his brethren were persecuted as Jesus was persecuted. Hananiah and his brethren were persecuted by Nebuchadnezzar; and Jesus, the people of the Jews persecuted. Hananiah and his brethren were cast into the furnace of fire, and it was cold as dew upon the righteous. Jesus also descended to the place of darkness, and burst its gates and brought forth its prisoners. Hananiah and his brethren came up from the furnace of fire, and the flame burned their accusers; and Jesus revived and came up from the midst of darkness, and His accusers and they that crucified Him shall be burned in flames at the end. When Hananiah and his brethren came up from the furnace, Nebuchadnezzar the King trembled and was amazed; and when Jesus arose from the abode of the dead, the people that crucified Him were terrified and trembled. Hananiah and his brethren worshipped not the image of the King of Babylon; and Jesus restrained the nations from the worship of dead images. Because of Hananiah and his brethren, the nations and languages glorified God Who had delivered them from the fire: and because of Jesus, the nations and oil languages shall glorify (God) Who delivered His Son, so that He saw no corruption. On the garments of Hananiah and his brethren the fire had no power; and on the bodies of the righteous, who have believed in Jesus, the fire shall have no power at the end.

20. Mordecai also was persecuted as Jesus was persecuted. Mordecai was persecuted by the wicked Haman; and Jesus was persecuted by the rebellious People. Mordecai by his prayer delivered his people from the hands of Haman; and Jesus by His prayer delivered His people from the hands of Satan. Morde-

cai was delivered from the hands of his persecutor; and Jesus was rescued from the hands of His persecutors. Because Mordecai sat and clothed himself with sackcloth, he saved Esther and his people from the sword; and because Jesus clothed Himself with a body and was illuminated, He saved the Church and her children from death. Because of Mordecai, Esther was well pleasing to the king, and went in and sat instead of Vashti, who did not do his will; and because of Jesus, the Church is well pleasing to God, and has gone in to the king, instead of the congregation which did not His Will. Mordecai admonished Esther that she should fast with her maidens, that she and her people might be delivered from the hands of Haman; and Jesus admonished the Church and her children (to fast), that she and her children might be delivered from the wrath. Mordecai received the honour of Haman, his persecutor; and Jesus received great glory from His Father, instead of His persecutors who were of the foolish People. Mordecai trod upon the neck of Haman, his persecutor; and as for Jesus, His enemies shall be put under His feet. Before Mordecai, Haman proclaimed, Thus shall it be done to the man, in honouring whom the king is pleased; and as for Jesus, His preachers came out of the People that persecuted Him, and they said:—This is Jesus the San of God. The blood of Mordecai was required at the hand of Haman and his sons; and the blood of Jesus, His persecutors took upon themselves and upon their children.

21. These memorials that I have written unto thee, my beloved, concerning Jesus Who was persecuted, and the righteous who were persecuted, are in order that those who to-day are persecuted for the sake of the persecuted Jesus, may be comforted, for He wrote for us and comforted us Himself; for He said:—If they have persecuted Me, they will also persecute you. And because of this they will persecute you, that ye are not of the world, even as I was not of it. For He wrote before for us:—Your fathers and your brothers and your family will deliver you up, and all men shall hate you for My name's sake. And again He taught us:—When they shall bring you before rulers and before magistrates, and before kings that hold the world, meditate not before the time what ye shall say, and how ye shall make defence; and I will give you a mouth and wisdom, that your enemies may not be able to overcome you, because it is not ye that speak, but the Holy Spirit of your Father; He shall speak in you. This is the spirit which spoke by the mouth of Jacob to Esau, his persecutor; and the spirit of wisdom which spoke before Pharaoh by the mouth of the persecuted Joseph; and the spirit which spoke by the mouth of Moses in all the prodigies which he did in the land of Egypt, and the spirit of knowledge which was given to Joshua, the son of Nun, when Moses laid his hand upon him, so that the nations which persecuted him came to a complete end before him; and the

spirit that uttered psalms by the mouth of the persecuted David, by which he used to sing psalms and soothe Saul his persecutor from the evil spirit; and the spirit which clothed Elijah, and through him reproved Jezebel and Ahab his persecutor; and the spirit which spoke in Elisha, and prophesied and made known to the king his persecutor about all that was to happen thereafter; and the spirit which was fervent in the mouth of Micaiah when he reproved Ahab his persecutor saying:—If thou shalt at all return back, the Lord hath not spoken by me; and the spirit which strengthened Jeremiah, so that he stood boldly, and by it reproved Zedekiah; and the spirit that preserved Daniel and his brethren in the land of Babylon; and the spirit that delivered Mordecai and Esther in the place of their captivity.

22. Hear, my beloved, these names of martyrs, of confessors, and of the persecuted. Abel was murdered, and his blood cried out from the earth. Jacob was persecuted, and fled and became an exile. Joseph was persecuted, and sold and cast into the pit. Moses was persecuted, and fled to Midian. Joshua the son of Nun was persecuted, and made war. Jephthah and Samson and Gideon and Barak, these also were persecuted. These are they of whom the blessed Apostle said:—Time fails me to narrate their victories. David also was persecuted at the hands of Saul, and he walked in the mountains and in dens, and in caves. Samuel also was persecuted, and mourned over Saul. Furthermore Hezekiah was persecuted, and bound up in affliction. Elijah was persecuted, and walked in the desert. Elisha was persecuted and became an exile; and Micaiah was persecuted, and cast into prison. Jeremiah was persecuted, and they cast him into the pit of mire. Daniel was persecuted, and cast into the pit of lions. Hananiah also and his brethren were persecuted, and cast into the furnace of fire. Mordecai and Esther and the children of their people were persecuted, at the hands of Haman. Judas Maccabaeus and his brethren were persecuted, and they also endured reproach. The seven brethren, sons of the blessed woman, endured torments by bitter scourgings, and were confessors and true martyrs, and Eleazar, aged and advanced in years as he was, proved a noble example and made (his) confession and became a true martyr.

23. Great and excellent is the martyrdom of Jesus. He surpassed in affliction and in confession all who were before or after. And after Him was the faithful martyr Stephen whom the Jews stoned. Simon (Peter) also and Paul were perfect martyrs. And James and John walked in the footsteps of their Master Christ. Also (others) of the apostles thereafter in divers places confessed and proved true martyrs. And also concerning our brethren who are in the West, in the days of Diocletian there came great affliction and persecution to the whole Church of God, which was in all their region. The Churches were

overthrown and uprooted, and many confessors and martyrs made confession. And (the Lord) turned in mercy to them after they were persecuted. And also in our days these things happened to us also on account of our sins; but also that what is written might be fulfilled, even as our Redeemer said:—These things are to be. The Apostle also said:—Also over us is set this cloud of confession; which (is) our honour, wherein many confess and are slain.

Demonstration XXII

Of Death and the Latter Times

1. The upright and righteous and good and wise fear not nor tremble at death, because of the great hope that is before them. And they at every time are mindful of death, their exodus, and of the last day in which the children of Adam shall be judged. They know that by the sentence of judgment death has held sway, because Adam transgressed the commandment; as the Apostle said:—Death ruled from Adam unto Moses even over those who sinned not, so that also upon all the children of Adam it passed, even as it passed upon Adam. And how did death rule from Adam unto Moses? Clearly, when God laid down the commandment for Adam, He warned him, and said:—On the day that thou shalt eat of the tree of the knowledge of good and evil, thou shalt die the death. So when he transgressed the commandment and ate of the tree, death ruled over him and over all his progeny. Even over those who had not sinned, even over them did death rule through Adam's transgression of the commandment.

2. And why did he say:—From Adam unto Moses did Death rule? And who is so ill-furnished with knowledge as to imagine that only from Adam to Moses has death had dominion? Yet let him understand from this that he said:—Upon all men it passed. Thus, upon all men it passed from Moses until the world shall end. Yet Moses preached that its kingdom is made void. For when Adam transgressed the commandment whereby the sentence of death was passed upon his progeny, Death hoped that he would bind fast all the sons of man and would be king over them for ever. But when Moses came, he proclaimed the resurrection, and Death knew that his kingdom is to be made void. For Moses said:—Reuben shall live and not die, and shall be in number. And when the Holy One called Moses from the bush he said thus to him:—I am the God of Abraham, of Isaac, and of Jacob. When Death heard this utterance, he trembled and feared and was terrified and was perturbed, and

knew that he had not become king for ever over the children of Adam. From the hour that he heard God saying to Moses:—I am the God of Abraham, of Isaac, and of Jacob, Death smote his hands together, for he learned that God is King of the dead and of the living, and that it is appointed to the children of Adam to come forth from his darkness, and arise with their bodies. And observe that our Redeemer Jesus also, when He repeated this utterance to the Sadducees, when they were disputing with Him about the Resurrection of the dead, thus said:—God is not (God) of the dead, for all are alive unto Him.

3. And that God might make known to Death that his authority is not for ever over all the progeny of the world, He translated Enoch to Himself, because he was well-pleasing, and made him deathless. And again He took up Elijah to heaven, and Death had no dominion over him. And Hannah said:—The Lord maketh to die and causeth to live; He bringeth down to Sheol and raiseth up. Furthermore Moses said as from the mouth of God:—I make to die and I cause to live. Again the Prophet Isaiah also said:—Thy dead shall live, and their dead bodies shall rise again; and the sleepers of the dust shall be awakened, and shall glorify Thee. When Death heard all these things, amazement seized him, and he sat him down in mourning.

4. And when Jesus, the slayer of Death, came, and clothed Himself in a Body from the seed of Adam, and was crucified in His Body, and tasted death; and when (Death) perceived thereby that He had come down unto him, he was shaken from his place and was agitated when he saw Jesus; and he closed his gates and was not willing to receive Him. Then He burst his gates, and entered into him, and began to despoil all his possessions. But when the dead saw light in the darkness, they lifted up their heads from the bondage of death, and looked forth, and saw the splendour of the King Messiah. Then the powers of the darkness of Death sat in mourning, for he was degraded from his authority. Death tasted the medicine that was deadly to him, and his hands dropped down, and he learned that the dead shall live and escape from his sway. And when He had afflicted Death by the despoiling of his possessions, he wailed and cried aloud in bitterness and said, "Go forth from my realm and enter it not. Who then is this that comes in alive into my realm?" And while Death was crying out in terror (for he saw that his darkness was beginning to be done away, and some of the righteous who were sleeping arose to ascend with Him), then He made known to him that when He shall come in the fulness of time, He will bring forth all the prisoners from his power, and they shall go forth to see the light. Then when Jesus had fulfilled His ministry amongst the dead, Death sent Him forth from his realm, and suffered Him not to remain there. And to devour Him like all the dead, he counted it not

pleasure. He had no power over the Holy One, nor was He given over to corruption.

5. And when he had eagerly sent Him forth and He had come forth from his realm, He left with him, as a poison, the promise of life; that by little and little his power should be done away. Even as when a man has taken a poison in the food which is given for (the support of) life, when he perceives in himself that he has received poison in the food, then he casts up again from his belly the food in which poison was mingled; but the drug leaves its power in his limbs, so that by little and little the structure of his body is dissolved and corrupted. So Jesus dead was the bringer to nought of Death; for through Him life is made to reign, and through Him Death is abolished, to whom it is said:—O Death, where is thy victory?

6. Therefore, ye children of Adam, all ye over whom Death has ruled, be mindful of Death and remember life; and transgress not the commandment as your first father did. O Kings, crowned with the diadem, remember Death, which will take away the diadems that are set upon your heads, and he shall be king over you till the time, when ye shall rise again for the judgment. O ye haughty and uplifted and proud, remember Death, which shall destroy your haughtiness, and dissolve the limbs, and separate the joints, and the body and its forms shall be given over to corruption. The lofty ones shall be brought low by Death, and the fierce and stern ones shall be buried away in his darkness. He shall take away all the pride, and they shall corrupt away and become dust, until the judgment. O ye rich, remember Death; for when the time shall come and ye shall draw nigh to him there, ye shall not use your wealth and possessions. He will not place dainty viands before you, nor will he prepare for you a rich banquet. There the body of the gluttons who used to live delicately shall be corrupted. They shall cease from their luxury and shall not remember it. There the worm shall consume their bodies, and they shall clothe themselves in darkness over their fair apparel. They remember not the ending of this world, that Death shall confound them when they descend to him. So they shall sit in oppression and in the shadow of death, and shall not remember this world, until the end shall be and they shall rise again for the judgment. O ye rapacious and extortioners and plunderers of your fellows, remember Death, and multiply not your sins; for in that place sinners repent not; and he who has plundered his fellows' goods shall not possess his own, but shall go to the place where man shall make no use of wealth. And he shall come to nought and pass away from his honour, but his sins shall be laid up against the day of judgment.

7. O ye that trust in this world, let this world be despised in your eyes; for ye are sojourners and aliens in the midst of it, and ye know not the day that ye shall be taken out of it. For suddenly shall Death come, and separate and lead away the loved children from their parents, and the parents from their darling children. He leads away for himself the precious only-begotten children, and their parents shall be deprived of them and shall come into contempt. He separates precious friends unto himself, and their beloved weep for them lamentably. He leads away and takes prisoners unto himself them that are desired for their beauty, that he may put to shame their forms and corrupt them. And those that are glorious in aspect he leads away to himself, and they become dust until the judgment. He leads away betrothed maidens from their spouses, and binds them captive in his bridal-chamber, in his place of gloom. He leads away and separates betrothed husbands from the virgins who were designed for them and betrothed in their name; and these shall sit in bitter mourning over them. He leads away and separates unto himself all the beautiful youths who supposed that even unto old age they would not see death. He leads away and gathers unto himself the loved infants of days, with whom their parents were not satiated. He leads away to himself the wealthy, the sons of luxury; And they leave their possessions as the waves of the sea. He leads away to himself the skilful artificers, who were raising up the world by their wonderful works. He leads away to himself the subtle and the wise, and they become simple, not distinguishing good from evil. He leads away to himself the richly endowed of this world, and their endowments are destroyed and shall not be established for ever. He leads away to himself the mighty and the great ones, and their might is brought low and weakened, and comes to an end. Them that were confident that their might would not be brought lower, in the day of death, men that are of lower degree than theirs gather together their bodies. They that trust that in their death they shall be buried with honour, it befalls them that the dogs devour them. And they that trust that they shall be buried in the place wherein they were born, know not but that in the land of their captivity they shall even be gathered (to the grave) with insult. They that trusted in their possessions, that they should give them in inheritance to their children, from them it is hidden that they shall be plundered by their enemies. Death leads away to himself the brave and the warriors. who thought to lay waste the great world. Death leads away them that adorn themselves with all pleasant things, and the burial of an ass befalls them when they are buried. Death rules over the unborn, and takes them captive to himself before they are born. Death leads away to himself them that are honoured with pomps, and they come into contempt when they descend to him, to the realm of darkness,

where there is no light. He is not ashamed before Kings (that are) crowned with the diadem. He is not abashed before the lofty and the fierce ones who lay waste the lands. Death respects not the persons of the honourable, nor does he receive a bribe from the rich. Death despises not the poor, nor does his soul scorn him that has nothing. Death honours not them that live in magnificence, nor with him are the good distinguished from the bad. He takes no account of the aged, rather than of children in respect of honour. The lords of prudence he makes without understanding, and them that used to make haste and vex themselves, in acquiring possessions there with him, these are stripped of their gains. He leads away to himself slaves and their masters; and there the masters are not honoured more than their servants. Small and great are there, and they hear not the voice of the oppressor. The slave who is freed from his master there pays no regard to him who used to oppress him. Death binds and makes captive to himself the keepers of prisoners, and the prisoners who were shut up. By means of Death the prisoners are released, and fear not again because of their oppressors.

8. They that live daintily fear death; but the afflicted look forward with hope that they shall be speedily taken away. All the rich tremble because of death; but the poor desire it, that they may rest from their labour. Death terrifies the mighty when they remember him; but the sick look forward with hope to him that through him they may forget their pains. Again the young children are afraid of death, for when it comes upon them they shall leave their pleasures; but the old men advanced in years pray for it, they that are in need of daily bread.

9. The sons of peace remember death; and they forsake and remove from them wrath and enmity. As sojourners they dwell in this world, and prepare for themselves a provision for the journey before them. On that which is above they set their thoughts, on that which is above they meditate; and those things which are beneath their eyes they despise. They send away their treasures to the place where there is no peril, the place where there is no moth, nor are there thieves. They abide in the world as aliens, sons of a far land; and look forward to be sent out of this world and to come to the city, the place of the righteous. They afflict themselves in the place of their sojourning; and they are not entangled or occupied in the house of their exile. Ever day by day their faces are set upwards, to go to the repose of their fathers. As prisoners are they in this world, and as hostages of the King are they kept. To the end they have no rest in this world, nor is (their) hope in it, that it will continue for ever. They that acquire possessions, rejoice not in them, and they that beget children, death fills them with sorrow. They that build cities, shall not be left in them;

and those that hasten and toil for anything, are in no wise to be distinguished from fools. O man without sense, whosoever he be whose trust is in this world!

10. Remember, my beloved, and compare and consider in thy mind, who is there of former generations who has been left in this world so as to continue for ever? Death has led away the former generations, the great ones and the mighty and the subtle. Who is there that acquired great possessions, and at the time when he departed took them with him? That which was gathered together from the earth returns back into its bosom; and naked does a man depart from his possessions. The wise, when they acquire goods, send some of them before them, as Job said:—My witnesses are heaven; and again:—My brethren and my lovers are with God. And our Lord commanded them that acquire possessions to make for themselves friends in heaven, and also to lay up treasures there.

11. Do thou also remember death, O wise scribe, that thy heart be not lifted up, so that thou shouldest forget the sentence of judgment. Death leaves not aside the wise, nor respects the persons of the subtle. Death leads away to himself the wise scribes, so that they forget that which they have learned, until the time comes in which all the righteous shall rise again.

12. In that place they shall forget this world. There they have no want; and they shall love one another with an abundant love. In their bodies there shall be no heaviness, and lightly shall they fly as doves to their windows. In their thoughts they shall not there remember wickedness at all, nor shall anything of uncleanness arise in their heart. In that place there shall be no natural desire, for there they shall be weaned from all appetites. There shall not arise in their heart anger or lasciviousness; also they shall remove from them all things that gender sins. Fervent in their heart will be the love of each other; and hatred will not be fixed within them at all. They shall have no need there to build houses, for they shall abide in light, in the mansions of the saints. They shall have no need of woven raiment, for they shall be clothed in eternal light. They shall have no need of food, for they shall recline at His table and be nurtured for ever. The air of that region is pleasant and glorious, and its light shines out, and is goodly and gladsome. Planted there are beautiful trees, whose fruits fail not, and whose leaves fall not. Their boughs are glorious, their perfume delightful, and of their taste no soul shall grow weary for ever. Spacious is the region, nor is it limited; yet its inhabitants shall see its distance even as that which is near. There the inheritance shall not be divided, and no man shall say to his fellow:—"This is mine and that is thine." They shall not be bound there in the desire of covetousness, nor shall they go astray there concerning remembrance. There a man shall not love his neighbour with especial reverence, but

abundantly shall they all love one another after one fashion. They shall not marry wives there, nor shall they beget children; nor shall there the male be distinguished from the female; but all shall be sons of their Father Who is in heaven; as the Prophet said:—Is there not one Father of us all; is there not one God Who created us?

13. And as regards that which I said; that there they shall not take wives, nor is male distinguished from female, our Lord and His Apostles have taught us. For our Lord said:—They that are worthy of that world, and of that resurrection from the abode of the dead, shall not take wives, nor shall (women) become wives to men; for they cannot die; but they are as the angels in heaven, and are the children of God. And the apostle said:—There is neither male nor female, neither bond nor free; but ye are all one in Jesus Christ. For, as for Eve, to spread abroad generation, God took her out from Adam, that she might become the mother of all living; but yet in that world there is no female; even as in heaven also there is no female, nor generation, nor use of concupiscence. In that place there is no deficiency, but fulness and perfection. The aged shall not die and the young shall not grow old. And it is in expectation of growing old and dying that young men take wives and beget children, that when the fathers shall have died the children may rise up in their stead. Now all these things have their use only in this world, for in that place there is no want, nor any deficiency, nor concupiscence, nor generation, nor ending, nor failure, nor death, nor termination, nor old age. There is neither hatred, nor wrath, nor envy, nor weariness, nor toil, nor darkness, nor night, nor falsehood. There is not in that place any want at all; but it is full of light, and life, and grace, and fulness, and satisfaction and renewal, and love, and all the good promises that are written but not yet sealed. For there is there that which eye hath not seen and ear hath not heard, and which hath not come up into the heart of man, that which is unspeakable and which a man cannot utter. And the Apostle said:—That which God hath prepared for them that love Him. Though men shall say much, they shall not be able to express it. That which eye hath not seen, they are unable to relate; and that which ear hath not heard, it is not right to speak of in such wise as to compare it with anything that the ear has heard and the eye has seen. And that which has not come up unto the heart, who is there dares to speak of it, as though it was like anything that has come up into the heart? But this is right for a speaker, to liken and call that place the abode of God, and the place of life, the perfect place, the place of light, the place of glory, the Sabbath of God, the day of rest, the repose of the righteous, the joy of the just, the abode and dwelling-place of the righteous and the holy, the place of our hope, the sure abode of our trust, the place of our treasure, the

place that shall assuage our weariness and remove our afflictions, and soothe our sighs. To these things it is right for us to liken, and thus to call, that place.

14. Again, Death leads away to himself kings, the founders of cities, who strengthen themselves in splendour. And he does not leave aside the Lords of the countries. Death leads away and takes captive to himself the avaricious who are not satisfied nor say "Enough"; and he is greedy for them with a greater greed than theirs. Death leads away to himself the despoilers who were not by their grace restrained from despoiling their fellows. Death leads away to himself the oppressors, and through death are they restrained from iniquity. Death leads away to himself the persecutors, and the persecuted have rest till they go to him. Death leads away to himself them that swallow up their fellows, and the down-trodden and oppressed have rest for a little until they themselves also are led away and go thither. Death leads away them that abound in meditations, and all they have thought upon is dissolved and brought to nought. Men meditate upon many matters, and death comes upon them suddenly, and they are led away; and thereafter they remember nothing that they have thought upon. There is one that makes plans for many years, and (the knowledge) is withheld from him that he shall not survive to-morrow. Some son of Adam is uplifted and vaunts himself over his fellow; and death comes upon him and brings to nought his vaunting. The rich man plans to add to his possessions, and he knows not that he shall not continue to possess even that which he has acquired. Death leads away to himself all the children of men, and binds them fast in his abode until the judgment. Also over those that have not sinned is he king, because of the sentence of judgment that Adam received for his sins.

15. And the Life-giver shall come, the Destroyer of Death, and shall bring to nought his power, from over the just and from over the wicked. And the dead shall arise with a mighty shout, and Death shall be emptied and stripped of all the captivity. And for judgment shall all the children of Adam be gathered together, and each shall go to the place prepared for him. The risen of the righteous shall go unto life, and the risen of the sinners shall be delivered unto death. The righteous who kept the commandment shall go, and shall not come nigh unto judgment in the day that they shall rise; as David asked, And bring not thy servant into judgment; nor will their Lord terrify them in that day.

16. Remember that the Apostle also said, We shall judge angels. And our Lord said to His disciples, Ye shall sit on twelve thrones, and judge twelve tribes of the house of Israel. And Ezekiel said concerning righteous men, that they shall judge Ahola and Aholibah. Since, then, the righteous are to judge the wicked, He has made clear concerning them that they shall not come into judgment. And as to what the apostles say, that We shall judge angels, hear,

and I will instruct thee. The angels who shall be judged by the apostles are the priests who have violated the law; as the Prophet said, The lips of the priest shall guard knowledge, and the law shall they inquire of his mouth; because he is the angel of the Lord, the most mighty. The angels who are the priests, of whose mouth the law is inquired, when they transgress the law, shall be judged at the last by the apostles, and the priests who observe the law.

17. And the wicked shall not arise in the judgment, nor sinners in the congregation of the righteous. And even as the righteous who are perfected in good works shall not come into the judgment to be judged, so of the wicked also whose sins are many, and the measure of whose offences is overflowing, it shall not be required that they should draw nigh unto the judgment, but when they have risen again they shall turn back to Sheol, as David said, The wicked shall turn back to Sheol, and all the nations that forget God. And Isaiah said, All the nations are as a drop from the bucket, and as the turning of the balance. And the isles as a grain of sand shall be cast away, and all the nations are esteemed as nothingness by Him. For destruction and the sword are they esteemed by Him. Therefore learn and be persuaded, that all the nations that know not God their Maker, are esteemed by God as nothingness, and shall not come nigh to judgment, but as soon as they have risen shall turn back to Sheol.

18. But all the rest of the world who are called sinners shall stand in the judgment and be rebuked. Those in whom there is a little shortcoming will the judge rebuke, and make known to them that they have offended. And He will give them the inheritance of life after the judgment. And understand that our Lord has made known to us in His Gospel, that every man according to his work shall receive his reward. He that received money, showed the increase on it. He whose pound or talent produced tenfold, received life, perfect, in nothing lacking. He whose pound or talent produced fivefold, received the half of ten. One was given a tenfold authority and one a fivefold. Now consider and see, that the increase of five is less than that of ten; and the labourers who demand the reward excel them that received it in silence. They who toiled all the day, with bold face receive the reward and demand it, in confidence that He will add more to them. While they who worked one hour receive it in silence, and know that through grace they receive mercy and life. The sinners whose sins are many shall be condemned by the place of judgment, and shall go into torments. And from that time and onwards, judgment shall rule over them.

19. Furthermore, hearken unto the Apostle who said, Every man according his work shall receive his reward. He that toiled little, shall receive according to his remissness; and he that made much speed, shall be rewarded according to

his speed. And Job also said, Far be it from God to do iniquity; and far be it from Him to do sin. For according to a man's works will He reward him, and a man shall receive according his ways. And also the Apostle said, Star excels star in brightness. So also is the resurrection of the dead. Therefore know that, even when men shall enter into life, yet reward shall excel reward, and glory shall excel glory, and recompense shall excel recompense. Degree is higher than degree; and light is more goodly than light in aspect. The sun excels the moon, and the moon is greater than the stars that are with her. And observe that the moon and the stars are also under the power of the sun, and their light is swallowed up in the splendour of the sun. And the sun has power along with the moon and the stars, that he may not abolish the night which has been separated from the day. And when the sun was created, he was called a luminary. And observe that the sun and the moon and the stars are all called luminaries; but luminary excels luminary. The sun obscures the light of the moon, and the moon likewise darkens the light of the stars; and star excels star in its light.

20. And understand (this) also, from that which is of this world, those who labour with toil, and from the hired men who work with their fellows. There are some who hire their fellow-men by day-wages, and (these) receive the wage of their toil; and there are some who are hired for the month, and compute and receive the wage for the time, at the time agreed. And the day-wage is distinguished from the monthly wage; and yearly exceeds monthly wage.

21. And also again, understand it from the authority that is in this world. There are some who please the king by their activity, and receive honour from those in authority. One receives a crown from the king, to become governor in one of the countries. And under the authority of another, the king places towns; and also he excels his inferiors in his attire. Some receive presents and gifts, and one honour is distinguished from another. There is one to whom the king gives the honour of being steward over all the treasury. Another, according to his lower condition, serves the king, and his authority is only to provide the daily food.

22. Also in respect of penalty, I say that all men are not equal. He that has done great wickedness is greatly tormented. And he that has offended not so much is less tormented. Some shall go into outer darkness, where there is weeping and gnashing of teeth. Others shall be cast into the fire, according as they deserve; for it is not written that they shall gnash their teeth, nor that there is darkness there. Some shall be cast into another place, a place where their worm shall not die, and their fire shall not be quenched, and they shall became an astonishment to all flesh. In the faces of others the door shall be

closed and the Judge will say to them:—I know you not. And consider that, as the reward for good deeds is not equal for all men, so it is also for evil deeds. Not in one fashion shall men be judged, but every man according to his works shall receive his requital, because the Judge is clothed in righteousness and regards not the persons of men.

23. And even as I have showed thee concerning the world, how one honour excels another, of those that kings and rulers of this world give to those beneath them; also concerning this I have showed thee, that even as kings have good gifts to give to those honoured by them, so also they have prisons and chains and fetters, which are various kinds of bonds. One man offends the king with a grievous offence, and without inquiry he is delivered over to death. Another offends, yet is not deserving of death; he is put in bonds until he is judged; and is chastised, and the king remits his offence. There is another whom the king has held in regard; and outside the prison house he is kept in freedom, without chains and without bonds. He that is put to death is distinguished from him that is bound; and the punishment of one exceeds that of another, according to the desert of his offence. But come thou to our Redeemer, Who said:—Many are the mansions in My Father's house.

24. My beloved, men who are inferior in understanding, dispute about this that I write to thee, and say:—"What is the place in which the righteous shall receive a good reward; and what is the place in which are torments, in which the wicked shall receive the punishments of their works?" O man that thinkest thus, I will ask thee, and tell thou me, why is death called death, and why is Sheol called Sheol? For it is written that when Korah and his companions made a schism against Moses, the earth opened her mouth and swallowed them up, and they went down alive into Sheol. Therefore that was the mouth of Sheol that was opened in the wilderness. David also said, The wicked shall turn back to Sheol. We say that to Sheol, in which Korah and his companions were swallowed up, thither shall the wicked be turned back. For God has power, if He chooses, to give inheritance of life in heaven, and if it please Him, in the earth. Jesus our Lord said, Blessed are the poor in spirit, for theirs is the kingdom of heaven. And to one of those who were crucified with Him, who believed on him He swore:—Thou shalt be with Me to-day in the garden Eden. And the Apostle said, When the righteous shall rise again, they shall fly upwards to meet our Redeemer. But, however, we say thus: That which our Redeemer said to us is true:—Heaven and earth shall pass away. And the Apostle said, Hope which is seen is not hope. And the Prophet said, The heavens shall pass away as smoke, and the earth as a garment shall wear away; and its inhabitants shall become like it. And Job said concerning those that

sleep, Till the heavens wear out, they shall not be aroused, nor shall they wake out of their sleep. From these things be thou persuaded that this earth, in which the children of Adam are sown, and the firmament that is over men, (even) that firmament which is set to divide the upper heavens from the earth and this life, shall pass away, and wear out, and be destroyed. And God will make a new thing for the children of Adam, and they shall inherit inheritances in the Kingdom of Heaven. If He shall give them inheritance in the earth, it shall be called the kingdom of heaven. And if in Heaven, it is easy for Him to do. For with the kings of the earth also, although each one of them abides in his own place, yet every place to which their authority extends, is called their kingdom. So the sun is a luminary set in the heaven, yet for every place to which its rays extend, its authority suffices, whether on sea or on land. And observe that the princes of the world also have banquetings and delights, and in every place or state into which they go, their banquetings are with them; and in whatever place pleases them, they make a prison-house. For the sun in twelve hours circles round, from the east unto the west; and when he has accomplished his course, his light is hidden in the night-time, and the night is not disturbed by his power. And in the hours of the night the sun turns round in his rapid course, and turning round begins to run in his accustomed path. As for the sun that is with thee, thou wise man, from thy childhood till the completion of thy old age, thou knowest not where he runs in the night-time, so as to circle round to the place of its course. Is it necessary for thee to inquire into those things that are hidden from thee?

25. These memorials I have written for our brethren and beloved, the children of the Church of God, that when these come into their hands in various places, and when they read in them, they may also remember my insignificance in their prayers, and may know that I am a sinner also, and fall short; but that this is my faith, that I have set forth from the beginning and written, in these chapters written (by me). Faith is the foundation, and upon faith (rest) the works that become it. And after Faith (I wrote) that there are two commandments of Love. And after Love, I have written of Fasting, in its demonstration also along with its works. And after Fasting, I wrote of Prayer in its fruit and in its works. And after Prayer, have written about War and about whatever Daniel wrote concerning the kingdoms. And after War, I have written of the exhortation for Monks. And after the Monks, I have written about Repentance. And after Repentance, I have written about the Resurrection of the dead. And after the Resurrection of the dead, I have written about Humility. And after Humility, I have written of the Pastors, the teachers. And after the Pastors, I have written about the Circumcision in which the people of the Jews

pride themselves. And after the Circumcision, I have written about the Passover, and about the fourteenth day. And after the Passover, I have written about the Sabbath, in which the Jews are puffed up. And after the Sabbath, I have written an Exhortation, on account of the dissension which happened in our days. And after the Exhortation, I have written about Meats, those that the Jews deem unclean. And after the Meats, I have written about the Gentiles, that they have entered in and become heirs instead of the original people. And after the Gentiles, I have written and proved that God has a Son. And after the Son of God, I have written against the Jews, who speak injuriously about Virginity. And after the apology about Virginity, I have written again Against the Jews, who say:—"It is appointed for us to be gathered together." And after that defence, I have written about Almsgiving to the Poor. And after the Poor, I have written a demonstration about The Persecuted. And after the Persecuted, I have written at the end about Death and the Last Times. These twenty-two discourses have I written according to the twenty-two letters of the alphabet. The first ten I wrote in the six hundred and forty-eighth year of the kingdom of Alexander the son of Philip the Macedonian, as is written in the end of them. And these twelve last I wrote in the six hundred and fifty-fifth year of the kingdom of the Greeks and of the Romans, which is the kingdom of Alexander, and in the thirty-fifth year of the Persian King.

26. These things I have written according to what I have attained to. But if anyone shall read these discourses, and find words that do not agree with his thought, he ought not to scorn them; because whatsoever is written in these chapters was not written according to the thought of one man, nor for the persuasion of one reader; but according to the thought of all the Church, and for the persuasion of all faith. If he shall read and hear with persuasion, it is well; and if not, it is meet for me to say that I wrote for those open to persuasion and not for mockers. And if again any reader should find words that are spoken by us in one fashion, and by another sage in another fashion, let him not be disturbed at this; for every man speaks to his hearers according to what he can attain to. So I, who have written these things, even if some of the words do not agree with what other speakers have said, yet say this; that those sages have spoken well, yet it seemed good to me to speak thus. And if any man shall speak and demonstrate to me about any matter, I will receive instruction from him without contention. Everyone who reads the sacred scriptures, both former and latter, in both covenants, and reads with persuasion, will learn and teach. But if he strives about anything that he does not understand, his mind does not receive teaching. But if he finds words that are too difficult for him, and he does not understand their force, let him say thus, "Whatsoever is

written is written well, but I have not attained to the understanding of it." And if he shall ask about the matters that are too hard for him of wise and discerning men who inquire into doctrine, then, when ten wise men shall speak to him in ten different ways about one matter, let him accept that which pleases him; and if any please not him, let him not scorn the sages; for the word of God is like a pearl, that has a beautiful appearance on whatever side you turn it. And remember, O disciple, what David said, From all my teachers have I learned. And the Apostle said:—Thou readest every Scripture that is in the Spirit of God. And prove everything; hold fast that which is good; and flee from every evil thing. For if the days of a man should be many as all the days of the world from Adam to the end of the ages, and he should sit and meditate upon the Holy Scriptures, he would not comprehend all the force of the depth of the words. And man cannot rise up to the wisdom of God; as I have written in the tenth discourse. But, however, the words of all speakers who do not take from the great treasure, are accursed and to be despised. For the image of the king (on his coin) is received wherever it goes; but (the coin) in which there is base metal, is rejected and is not received. And if any one should say, "These discourses were spoken by such an one;" let him carefully learn that to be careful to inquire about the speaker is not commanded him. I also according to my insignificance have written these things, a man sprung from Adam, and fashioned by the hands of God, a disciple of the Holy Scriptures. For our Lord said:—Every one that asketh receiveth, and he that seeketh findeth, and for him that knocketh it shall be opened. And the prophet said:—I will pour out my spirit upon all flesh in the last days, and they shall prophesy. Therefore whoever shall read anything that I have written above, let him read with persuasion, and pray for the author as a brother of the Body; that through the petition of all the Church of God; his sins may be forgiven. And let whoever reads understand what is written:—Let him that hears the word, communicate to him that causes him to hear, in all good things. And again it is written, The sower and the reaper shall rejoice together. And Every man according to his labours shall receive his reward. And There is nothing hidden that shall not be revealed to every man.

Made in the USA
Columbia, SC
03 December 2019